AF182618

SpringerBriefs in Criminology

Translational Criminology

For further volumes:
http://www.springer.com/series/11178

About this Series

Has research made a difference to criminal justice practices and policies? Evidence-based crime policy is not just about rigorously generating a robust supply of rigorous research to find out "what works" in terms of justice interventions or "what explains" crime or offending. Evidence-based crime policy means that this supply should be attuned to the demand for research, and that research must be converted to meaningful forms and implemented with fidelity in order for practice to be receptive to science. But how does this actually happen?

An important concept in the field of evidence-based crime policy is translational criminology, or how, why, whether, and under what conditions research is converted to, and used, in practice. This Springer Brief series on translational criminology brings to both the academe and criminal justice world examples of how research becomes practice and policy, and whether research has made an impact. Each brief is written by top scholars and/or practitioners in the field who describe specific examples of how a body of research became practice (or didn't) and the lessons learned from the endeavor.

Leslie W. Kennedy • Yasemin Irvin-Erickson
Alexis R. Kennedy

Translational Criminology and Counterterrorism

Global Threats and Local Responses

Springer

Leslie W. Kennedy
School of Criminal Justice
Rutgers University
Newark, NJ, USA

Yasemin Irvin-Erickson
School of Criminal Justice
Rutgers University
Newark, NJ, USA

Alexis R. Kennedy
Fort Collins, CO, USA

ISSN 2194-6442 ISSN 2194-6450 (electronic)
ISBN 978-1-4614-5555-4 ISBN 978-1-4614-5556-1 (eBook)
DOI 10.1007/978-1-4614-5556-1
Springer New York Heidelberg Dordrecht London

Library of Congress Control Number: 2014940765

Printed on acid-free paper

Springer is part of Springer Science+Business Media (www.springer.com)

Contents

Abbreviations

AQT	Al Qaeda Turkey
ATAC	Anti-Terrorism Academy
CCTV	Closed-Circuit Television
CIA	Central Intelligence Agency
CTC	Counter-Terrorism Committee
DARPA	Defense Advanced Research Project Agency
ECPAT	End Child Prostitution Child Pornography and Trafficking of Children for Sexual Purposes
ECHR	European Court of Human Rights
ETA	Homeland and Freedom
FARC	Revolutionary Armed Forces of Colombia
FEMA	Federal Emergency Management System
HFLC	High frequency low consequence
HIDTA	High Intensity Drug Trafficking Area
IAEA	International Atomic Energy Agency
ICCPR	International Covenant on Civil and Political Rights
ICE	Immigration and Custom's Enforcement
(ICE)DRO	Detention and Removal Operations
ICS	Incident Command System
ICT	Information and Communication Technologies
IDB	Turkish Office of the Director of Intelligence
INS	Immigration and Naturalization Service
IRA	Irish Republican Army
ISP	Internet Service Providers
KLA	Kosovo Liberation Army
LAN	Local Area Network
LFHI	Low Frequency High Impact
MIT	Turkish National Intelligence Organization
NASA	National Aeronautics and Space Administration
NCIS	National Criminal Intelligence Service
NCSA	National Cyber Security Alliance

NGO	Nongovernmental Organizations
NIPC	National Infrastructure Protection Agency
NPT	Nuclear Non-Proliferation Treaty
NSA	National Security Agency
OECD	Organization for Economic Cooperation and Development
PKK	Kurdish Worker's Party
PLC	Programmable Logic Controller
RTM	Risk Terrain Modeling
SMB	Service Message Board
SOC-UM	Safeguarding Our Children—United Mothers
TERSH	Taksim Education and Research State Hospital
TRAC	Transactional Records Access Clearinghouse
UNODC	United Nations Office of Drugs and Crime
UNSC	United Nations Security Council
WHO	World Health Organization

Translational Criminology and Counterterrorism: Global Threats and Local Responses

Part I. Global Risk Assessment and the Impact on Local Response

Introduction

This "brief" offers an overview of how analysis of crime and terrorism can be evaluated both in terms of research to practice (what we interpret as "translational") and combining the two literatures relating to global and local effects. The complications that come from merging two sets of literature, drawing from security studies and criminology, may create challenges for the reader unfamiliar with one or the other. However, our take on this series is that it is supposed to introduce readers to different literature, not necessarily expound on it in detail. If one is interested in pursuing this topic further, references are included.

In writing this brief, we viewed the series as directed towards researchers who are trying to make sense of their work in terms of its application to key areas of counterterrorism and crime. We offer a framework for our studies, what we refer to as a "common methodology," to help us sort out steps in the risk assessment process used by different agencies to manage policies and programs addressing emerging threats. We use case studies that provide examples, or evidence, of how the translational approach works using the common methodology. While this is not a "how-to" book, the final section deals with the "practical" steps that researchers can take to communicate their results. This guidance should be useful for both researchers and practitioners. The whole approach we advocate demands that one addresses evidence before moving forward to practice. Upon completion of this brief, the reader will come away with a framework to understand risk assessment using this translational approach.

L.W. Kennedy et al., *Translational Criminology and Counterterrorism: Global Threats and Local Responses*, SpringerBriefs in Criminology, DOI 10.1007/978-1-4614-5556-1_1, © The Author 2014

The Role of Translational Criminology and Counterterrorism in the Study of Global Threats

Criminologists worked for years to encourage practitioners and policy makers to allow greater access to data, thus facilitating academic research. This promoted the development of investigation into law enforcement practice. As a consequence, there is increased involvement by agencies in evidence-based practices. The successes that came from increased cooperation and collaborations are noteworthy because they prompted a discussion around how these types of partnerships and exchanges can be standardized and broadened.

Laub (2011) defines the point of contact between researchers and practitioners as "translational criminology," which he describes as having the goal of breaking down barriers by creating a dynamic interface between basic research and practice. He goes on to say that translational criminology:

> … is not just about finding evidence that something works; it is figuring out why it works and how to implement the evidence in real-world settings. Moreover, this facet of translational criminology places a priority on applicability—that is, on research with the potential for real-world implementation, something that is especially attractive in an era of limited resources (Laub, 2011, p. 17).

This translational process can be looked at in light of the demands placed on law enforcement to anticipate and prevent all types of crimes from occurring by broadening their data analysis and forecasting techniques. The challenges faced in this area of inquiry will be the topic of this brief. One focus in this review is how translational approaches can be applied to the problems posed to law enforcement at the local and state level by global threats of crime and terrorism.

Translational approaches require a plan to be effective. Simply assuming that research will have an immediate and obvious application in crime response leads nowhere. There has to be a clear set of steps involved in outlining how we translate data analysis to action. This can take on a number of different shapes but we believe that it should revolve around a set of principles that form agreed-upon practice, that can be applied in different jurisdictions, and that can be used to solve different types of problems.

This review will be guided by the insights related to what Van Brunschot and Kennedy (2011) describe as "dynamic security states" that are created at the intersection of hazards (or threats), resources, and exposure. Each of these security states constitutes an effort to balance harm (or the possibility of harm) with the application of resources (such as knowledge and money). Over time, at different stages of the event, Van Brunschot and Kennedy argue, the balance can change. This happens because prevention measures are taken prior to an incident, there is reduced exposure during an incident, or prevention measures are taken based on what was learned from previous incidents.

At the same time, when looking at hazards, these balance calculations can vary greatly. Such variation may lead to the requirement of different resources and interventions developed according to the type of hazard, but also according to the stage of the event. The consequences of all these factors influence the risk balance calculation that ultimately is performed to judge appropriate response (p. 13).

Using this idea of security states and combining all parts of the process from threats to responses provides a framework that demonstrates how research and practice are interconnected. Balance is achieved from sensible interventions and is measured against the reality of hazards. The translational theme suggests that gathered information converges from systematic observation to actionable response.

We will begin by discussing a common methodology that can be used to articulate the translational process into operational steps. This common methodology is drawn from an analysis of the ways in which agencies in public health, disaster, and counterterrorism formulate risk assessments and translate these into strategic interventions: moving from data to action (Kennedy, Marteache, & Gaziarifoglu, 2011). Our review is set in the context of the global security debates, specifically terrorism and cyber-threats. We present the issues related to preventing, analyzing, and mitigating these crimes, emphasizing the need for a clear understanding of how global changes impact local communities and reframe the challenges to security.

Considering the Translational Steps in Risk Assessment in the Context of Globalization and Its Impacts on Local Security

Globalization is touted as a positive step for humanity. Its benefits are extolled in the ways in which it improves economies, broadens cultural diversity, and empowers individuals (Ferguson & Mansbach, 2012). The downsides of globalization are also well documented, ranging from concerns of crime, the spread of disease, and environmental degradation (Scholte, 2005). In this new world, characterized by Beck (1992) as a "risk society," law enforcement and agency control shifts from a focus on controlling risky behavior to a concentration on managing risky populations. This emphasis matches the new ways in which we talk about what is dangerous and what is not. It serves as a defining feature in how we respond to the hazards that we face.

In the past, the nation state had the responsibility to maintain sovereignty, territoriality, centralized authority, and monopoly of legitimate force. However, the emergence of international organizations and nongovernmental organizations (NGOs) that address international development suggests a broad impact of globalization on cross-national governance. Yet, these initiatives are halting and poorly coordinated (if at all). Further, the impact of globalization on contemporary national governments is not very well understood (most importantly, as we will see, in the area of security).

Ferguson and Mansbach (2012) observe that in the last few decades, individual, state, and global security are merging because people are searching for a sense of collective action that all too often is not available. As a result, insecurity continues to build, although Ferguson and Mansbach point out that this unease has been mitigated as the threat of nuclear attack has obviously lessened since the end of the Cold War (p. 40). This does not mean that people are free of fear; rather the threats have become more diffused than before. More importantly, the threats to security appear to be more keenly felt in local rather than global terms, repeating a theme that globalization means the "nearness of distant places" or "distant proximities" (Rosenau, 2003). In using this concept, Rosenau suggests that the world, with globalization of technology, travel, and communication, condensed interactions and influenced local cultures. As Ikenberry (2003) explains:

> The globalizing forces of the information revolution, free markets, and expanding American influence interact with the localizing forces of nationalism, religious fundamentalism, and anti-Americanism (n.p.).

The recent concerns over the world financial crisis, fears of cross-border crime and terrorism, and the reemergence of identity politics reversed the effects of globalization. This involved restricting the movement of people and things through tightening controls, increased security, and greater local surveillance of external threats (Ferguson & Mansbach, 2012). Ferguson and Mansbach suggest that this reinforcing of local interest is not really surprising as globalization and local interests can be self-reinforcing. In responding to the implication that globalizing trends in transnational law or economics do not necessarily result in the loss of local controls, they state, "What it does not mean is that the local has been erased or absorbed by the global. In other words, the global and the local are completely related and may simultaneously compete with or reinforce one another" (p. 138).

It should be noted that this relationship is an uneasy one, as the source of global threats may be out of the control of the local authorities. It is argued, for example, that the spread of democracy and human rights is a natural concomitant of global markets, cultures, and values. However, critics believe that globalization, in fact, increases inequality and poverty as some parts of the world are left out of the market (Scholte, 2005). This has the effect of fostering separatist movements, supporting terrorists, and reinforcing sectarianism. Further, global corporations often manage their operations at the expense of local concerns, including poor working conditions, environmental pollution, and threats to personal safety.

Globalization promotes easy and efficient movement of goods, services, people, and ideas around the world. Security concerns seek to control and sometimes block this easy movement. Globalization moves capital into areas where workers are available at the most cost-effective level to produce goods that can be transshipped anywhere in the world. Security concerns emerge when companies face local expectations about working conditions and pay and have continuous worry about assets, patent infringement, and the like. This leads to the development of supranational organizations that administer laws to enhance cross-national security, but this is administered haphazardly and without consistent standards of enforcement.

Cha (2000) talks about "intermestic" security, the mixing of international and domestic security threats. In responding to threats, national security forces have not kept up with globalization demands. Unilateral actions against global threats are often hard to mobilize and difficult to manage in terms of an agreed upon mission. In addition, in his article written before the World Trade Center attacks, he predicts the post-9/11 partnerships between local law enforcement and national security agencies (p. 393).

For security to be effective, it must be scalable, that is, factors that influence the sense of safety on the local level have a direct effect on the national and international level and vice versa, an outcome of the interdependence discussed above. This is probably best illustrated in the recent attempts to combine local law enforcement in the national fight against terrorism, including the decision on the part of the New York Police Department to set up international intelligence offices to tackle terrorism. Problems arise, though, as information collected nationally and internationally cannot be freely exchanged with the local police departments. The filter of secrecy creates a roadblock for these agencies in scaling their operations and agreeing on similar responses to security threats. Without an integrated response, there will always be a problem in coordinating decisions and matching policies.[1]

An unsettling aspect of the 9/11 incident for Americans relates to the fact that an extra-national attack was launched on US soil against infrastructure that should have been safe. The point of the onslaught was to show that the safety that comes from globalization (keeping insecure factors outside one's borders) could be breached. This lack of security of the American population and infrastructure became the direct focus of US leaders in response to the terrorist attacks. However, care must also be given in addressing what it is that needs to be secured. While a great deal of concern is directed at the safe manufacture and movement of goods and people, much of what is moved (money, ideas, influence) can be transported through safe channels on the Internet or secure financial networks (intranets). As we will see, increasingly, these pathways offer new opportunities for exploitation and challenges to protection.

It could be argued that on the surface, the actual effects of 9/11 on reducing the growth of globalization may not be as expected. In fact, they may have both accelerated globalization and increased the demand for local security, demonstrating the interdependence discussed by Ferguson and Mansbach. Barriers to free migration were put in place after these attacks in response to concerns about cross-national organized crime, money laundering, and terrorism. However, this has not really stopped multinational companies from increased reliance on international supply chains, and expanding global manufacture, service, and distribution networks.

Global threats cannot simply be managed through increased surveillance and more aggressive law enforcement. Davis suggests that the unequal development of state powers to cope with the effects of the easy movement of capital across borders leads to feelings of resentment and deprivation (Davis, 2003, p. 4). Further, countries that are economically disadvantaged become increasingly vulnerable to the threats of destabilization that may emerge from poverty, religious radicalism, or divisions in political ideology. Davis suggests that governments must become alert to these problems and be more active in preventing the negative consequences of the

[1] See Anarumo, 2011 for a discussion of the views of US local law enforcement towards getting valid intelligence about terrorism threats and the challenges that they face in prevention and response.

globalizing process. Beyond this, more attention must be paid to surveying and monitoring health issues, poverty, and religious fanaticism. Her prescriptions for government response include improved education, health and employment insurance, and the advancement of social and physical infrastructure. Not doing these things, Davis asserts, will lead to increased insecurity. However, she maintains that it is clear that local governments cannot do this alone (p. 3).

There should be a much more concerted effort to supplement local and regional efforts to deal with globalization (Davis, 2003). This can be done at the transnational level through the development of collective international decision-making processes that bring together governments, NGOs, private companies, and multilateral institutions to respond to and develop strategies around security (p. 6). Attention can be paid to the most obvious global threats, including smuggling of nuclear material, trafficking guns and people, and protecting countries from the spread of disease (p. 2). Security can be assured through the systematic development of economic well-being across countries, a role that these types of global decision-making structures could facilitate (p. 5). We will explore how these types of intergovernmental responses work in our review of the case studies. Local responses to threats must be coordinated with national and international agencies and must go beyond a simple response that involves intervention through law enforcement alone.

In summary, globalization has created a new security reality. This needs to be confronted by agencies that will see the product of the new threats appear as local events demanding prevention and response. An important aspect of this new reality involves the extent to which a coordinated response can be developed to identify, respond to, and manage these threats. This is the focus of the discussion in the next section, where we consider the extent to which we can apply a "common methodology" to risk analysis leading to standardized responses across different areas of concern.

Part II. Understanding Uncertainty, Intelligence, and Risk: Creating a Common Methodology to Respond to Emerging Global Threats

Overcoming Uncertainty

Some would argue that the best way to deal with the uncertainty of potential negative outcomes is to take no chances at all. This view has been termed the "precautionary principle" which dictates that in public and private policies, we do not allow for even the remote possibility of any harmful effect (Van Brunschot & Kennedy, 2008). In more direct terms, a certain type of activity is restricted unless research has proven that it does not have harmful effects. According to the Wingspread conference in Racine, WI, in 1998, the precautionary principle suggests that, "...when an activity raises threats of harm to human health or the environment, precautionary measures should be taken even if some cause and effect relationships are not fully established scientifically" (Appell, 2001, p. 1). The precautionary principle, therefore, does not rely on conclusive evidence, but rather is motivated by particular values over and above conclusive (or nonexistent) evidence. Appell explains:

> In other words, actions taken to protect the environment and human health take precedence. Therefore, some advocates say, governments should immediately ban the planting of genetically modified crops, even though science cannot yet say definitively whether they are a danger to the environment or to consumers (p. 1).

The precautionary principle is applied even if there is little evidence to show that these harms are likely to occur under all circumstances. Hence, following this logic, there is merit in providing security funding against terrorism to all constituencies in a country, even though certain areas have a remote likelihood of being attacked. Taken further, the lack of evidence of these areas being targets does not mitigate the damage that would be done if they became targets.

Is it possible for us to anticipate all negative consequences of our actions? Obviously, we can't. This doesn't mean that we give up the belief that, with more knowledge and technology, we can improve our management of risks, as evidenced by our successes in disease control, for example. It is never possible to completely eradicate the threats that come from determined criminals or terrorists. This may lead us to decide that we are better off safe than sorry. However, in confronting the reality that we cannot always be perfectly safe, we can understand more about what contributes to security through preparedness, prevention, and response. These tools are what we use to balance the risk we face in our lives (Van Brunschot & Kennedy, 2008).

In responding to uncertainty, we set out to assess the risks that do exist. We begin by collecting information about threats, assessing vulnerabilities, and computing strategies to manage risks. An important means by which we gather this information is through the collection and analysis of data and intelligence.

Information, Intelligence, and Accountability

Transparency plays an important role in the security arena. The police, for years, resisted any efforts to lift secrecy on crime statistics but have since relented. They now understand that transparency is actually helpful in managing their problems and enlisting support from the public, both in responding to crime and also in justifying resources for their organizations. In the area of national public security, this transparency is less forthcoming, however, and there are efforts to actually restrict access to data and information, hiding it behind the shield of "top secret intelligence".

How do public agencies use intelligence, gleaned from surveillance, informants, public sources, and investigations, to judge threat and undertake interventions? The recent case which revealed the extent to which massive amounts of phone and e-mail records of American citizens was collected by National Security Agency (NSA) demonstrates how problematic this demand for secrecy is when contrasted against civil rights and privacy concerns. The need for data is a central aspect of the translational approach. However, balancing this necessity against a clearly defined set of rules for data collection becomes a paramount concern.

Intelligence is information (or data) that has relevance for action and, for this brief, the action involved is the promotion of security. Intelligence also involves forecasting and providing information to direct future actions (Herman, McDonald, & Mastny, 2006; Treverton, Jones, Boraz, & Lipscy, 2006). Intelligence is intended to forecast future events and guide decision-makers in developing strategies to protect the public from danger. However, intelligence can be flawed and decisions can be made off the mark. More importantly, intelligence may be used to justify actions that are not factually supportable, causing people to question the accuracy of the predictions and the motives of those making the decisions.

Increasingly, intelligence is turned inward on nations, leading to a new era of managing threats from outside and from within borders, a theme that we see recurring in our discussion of the threats of cybercrime and terrorism.[2] Recently, the US intelligence community has come under attack by those who believe that their claims regarding the need for enhanced security have been used to justify increasingly costly and ineffective security apparatuses. One of the most vocal of these critics is Jon Mueller (2006), whose book, *Overblown*, makes a detailed study of the US government counterterrorism policies and reports and finds them unsustainable.

Another critic, Ian Lustick (2006), writes about the phantom threats that national security agencies are looking for but cannot find. Their views suggest that the organization of security response is self-perpetuating and not justified by real evidence of danger, certainly not on the scale that matches the resources that are demanded to respond to these threats. Further, the threat is used to justify all sorts of other positions in government that are, again, not substantiated through evidence.

[2] See footnote 16 in Treverton et al. (2006).

The particular form of evidence that is missing, these critics repeat, is the lack of a subsequent attack in the US since the 9/11 bombing.

Research produced by the National Consortium for the Study of Terrorism and Responses to Terrorism (START) center at the University of Maryland describes a continuous downward trend in incidents in the US in the last decade (START, 2011). In a recently published article, LaFree, Yang, and Crenshaw (2009) analyze a comprehensive database of almost 17,000 terrorist attacks worldwide from START. They conclude that even though the groups mounting these attacks proclaimed the US as their major target, they were only successful in launching five operations on US soil and less than 5 % of the attacks were directed at US targets outside of the US (p. 457).

These criticisms of excessive government responses are countered by law enforcement agencies. The Federal Bureau of Investigation (FBI) (2008) points out that, while it may be true that nothing has occurred since the World Trade Center attacks, this is largely due to the fact that government and nongovernment agencies are much more vigilant and more effective in deterring attacks than before. However, this assertion is made in the context of an opaque climate of intelligence where, even if the US was continuously thwarting attacks, the public would likely not be told the details because of the classified nature of the information that is collected and analyzed.

The role of intelligence in providing security is a complex one, as it requires secrecy. But, it also must be used in a way that provides warning. If we are left without the wherewithal to convince the public of the value of intelligence, we likely won't have any and the warnings will be hard to formulate. At the same time, warnings without credibility are of little or no use. In a connected way, intelligence agencies that fail to identify threats are quickly compromised. Therefore, we need to use the "trust me" stance in developing intelligence. However, the ongoing support for resources in managing security, in the absence of threats and warnings, is likely not sustainable.

Intelligence runs the risky line of forecasting the future based on a creative assessment of past behavior and suggestions about how things will eventually transpire. Many efforts have been made to standardize the intelligence process but the complexity of dealing with the dangers posed by non-state actors and hidden agents makes this type of intelligence hard to manage. Also, the fast moving aspects of modern communication, while useful in extending influence and gathering information, is itself used in creating threats and insecurity. The information that is used may mean different things to different people depending on their socialization, their experiences, and their future interests. It is in this realm of conflicting messages that a great deal of confusion develops around global security. In the next section, we present a strategy that can help assess the elements of risk, responses to threats, and ways of increasing global and local security.

Using Common Methodology in the Risk Assessment of Global Threats

In the words of William O. Jenkins, Jr., the Director of Homeland Security and Justice Issues, in testimony to a Congressional hearing in 2007:

> A risk management approach entails a continuous process of mitigating risk through a series of actions, including setting strategic goals and objectives, assessing risk, evaluating alternatives, selecting initiatives to undertake, and implementing and monitoring those initiatives (Jenkins, 2007, p. 26).

Jenkins alerts us to the fact that the risk assessment process cannot simply be one in which there are broad guidelines applied to defining risks. What is important to consider is that all of these risk assessments, to be useful, must include an element of accountability built into them. That is, there must be a clear set of rules about who is responsible for a problem and a set of guidelines about what they should do to respond to the threats that appear.

Defined as "common methodology," risk analysis and response can be organized into three parts: (1) risk assessment, (2) decision-making, and (3) risk management (Kennedy et al., 2011, p. 33). By breaking an event down into these three phases, we can dissect the strategies used by agencies and policy makers faced with emerging threats. Analysts have found that it is more effective to examine a threat in terms of factors occurring before, during, and after an incident, and not the single incident alone (p. 33). By adding a time dimension to an event and examining the factors that contributed to its danger, agencies are better prepared to prevent, mitigate, respond to, and control hazards. Using this approach allows us to operationalize the progression of the translational process as we move from data to action. In this section, we summarize the three steps of the common methodology.

Risk Assessment

Before an event occurs, risks are assessed and information is gathered regarding uncertainty, exposure, and vulnerability of a population to a specific threat. In addition, analysis is performed to determine the types of data needed for accurate threat assessment and the sources where these data can be collected (we will discuss these data issues below). During this phase, risks are evaluated to apprehend the likelihood and consequences of emerging threats. Furthermore, agencies attempt to define and understand the threat, gathering intelligence to pass on to higher-ranking decision-makers. The cost of action is weighed against the cost of inaction, from an economic, political, and social standpoint. Agencies create priorities, including who or what should be protected. At this point, resources including staff, data, supplies, food, and weapons must be examined to prepare for the impending catastrophe.

More specifically, as described by Kennedy et al. (2011), the following questions should be asked by agency personnel during this phase of the common methodology:

- What type of threat or hazard are we facing?
- What types of data are needed?
- What are the sources of information available?
- What is the level of certainty that the event will occur?
- How vulnerable are we? Why?
- How exposed are we? Why?
- How does the flow of information from the local to a higher level work? Are there specific protocols to follow? (p. 34).

Threats can be abstract or identifiable. An example of an abstract threat is the threat of terrorism, in which little is known regarding who will commit a future terrorist act, where it will take place, or when it will occur (Van Brunschot & Kennedy, 2011, p. 11). These threats are especially difficult to understand and predict and many agencies use policies that generalize high-risk suspicion to a group of people (from individuals who may be identified as active members of an insurgent or terrorist group or an activity such as people boarding planes).

Identifiable threats are those that are recognizable, in the sense that authorities have information regarding the who, what, where, and when relating to an event. An example of an identifiable threat is the reporting requirement under Megan's Law or the Sexual Offender Act of 1994. Although different states have different variations of the law, generally, if a convicted sex offender is released from prison, he/she must register his/her address with the local police department. This information is then distributed to the public (Zgoba, Witt, Dalessandro, & Veysey, 2008). While this person may not re-offend, his/her history and psychology makes him/her riskier than someone without the same disposition.

Analyzing a risk in this way is essential to understanding the true threat that may be faced. If the likelihood of an adverse event occurring is high, as was the case with Hurricane Sandy hitting the coast of New Jersey and New York, a chain of command is put into place to ease communication between decision-makers and those working on the street. Volunteers and professionals are given specific jobs in logistics, communications, transportation, healthcare, etc. If the threat requires people to move, as it did with Hurricane Sandy, communication with the public is essential to effectively evacuate the area of high risk (e.g., the New Jersey Shore, lower Manhattan, Staten Island, and Long Island) and to minimize the loss of life.

Risk assessment changes when an adverse event is actually taking place. At this time, the probability of the event occurring is equal to one, although the chances of where the event occurs, who it affects, and how bad is the damage are yet to be determined. After an event occurs, risk is reassessed to determine the present condition of vulnerability and threats to security, as well as the future probability of a similar event occurring. Once again, data and information are gathered to analyze the factors related to the event. Furthermore, analysts will collect data regarding the reactions of the victims, the responding agency, and the public (Sacco & Kennedy, 2002, p. 63). With these data, agencies and policy makers can better understand what victims need in terms of medical help (both physical and mental). They can also revisit the decisions made in order to analyze the effectiveness of the operations.

During the manhunt involved in identifying and capturing the perpetrators of the Boston bombings, which occurred on April 15, 2013, law enforcement enlisted the help of the media to track down the suspects. Information about the suspects came first from an eyewitness and victim of the bombings, who gave a description of a man placing something under the bleachers where the victim was sitting (Loder & Deprez, 2013). Through surveillance, including photos and videos taken by the public, analysts were able to gather enough data to ascertain that the Tsarnaev brothers could be responsible for the bombings. As discussed below, public involvement through technology (i.e., camera phones and online communities including Twitter, Facebook, and Reddit) is a useful, although at times unreliable, source of information for law enforcement agencies.

Decision-Making

If an agency, through the risk assessment phase, determines that a threat is real and imminent, the organization in charge enters the decision-making phase of operations. During this time, strategists and policy makers decide how to face the emerging threat. Throughout the decision-making phase of the common methodology, the following questions are asked:

- Who is in charge of evaluating the risk at this level and making decisions? How is that authority established?
- What is the risk assessment that has been received from the local level? Has the risk been reassessed at a higher level? With what result?
- What are the priorities?
- What are the available resources? How can they be allocated effectively?
- Once the decisions about how to face the threat are made, how are they communicated? To whom? How is that established?
- Is monitoring foreseen as a source of data for constant decision-making? Are there protocols of reexamination of decisions according to new information in place? (Kennedy et al., 2011, p. 34).

An organization, first, establishes who is in charge and who will make the tough decisions regarding the prevention, mitigation, and cleanup once such a disaster occurs. These decisions may include evacuation; deploying police or military force; and/or actions that may affect people economically, such as temporarily closing down businesses. As risk assessment continues throughout the decision-making phase, leaders must understand how a threat may have local, state, national, and global consequences (Kennedy et al., 2011, p. 33). Based on these reviews, agencies will make decisions regarding what are the priorities, what are the available resources, and how these resources can be allocated effectively to minimize damage. Importantly, communication and monitoring systems must be put in place so that orders can be received and followed correctly and decisions can be reevaluated as threats change.

After the event, policy makers and agency leaders make decisions regarding the mitigation, reconstruction, and continued protection of the area in which the crisis occurred. In the week after the Boston bombings, local, state, and national police forces worked together to find and take down the Tsarnaev brothers. After being spotted at a 7–11, MIT campus police and the Boston police attempted to apprehend the brothers, resulting in one officer and the older brother, Tamerlan, being killed. Dzhokhar, the younger brother, was injured but escaped (Sullivan, Barr, & Zezima, 2013). Despite the disastrous result of this first encounter, intelligence agencies were able to pinpoint where Dzhokhar was located. Decisions were made including requiring locals to stay in their homes while police continued to search. Boston was slowly shut down for the day, as the manhunt continued through the evening. When it was discovered that the suspect was hiding in a civilian's boat, parked in his backyard in the Boston suburb of Watertown, the injured suspect was quickly apprehended and brought to the hospital under custody.

After Dzhokhar Tsarnaev was finally apprehended, decision-makers were tasked with establishing policies to prevent terrorist attacks from occurring at the future marathon races being held throughout the US. Two weeks after the Boston marathon incident, the Long Island marathon took place. It was decided that the race would not be canceled since, during the risk assessment phase, it was determined that the risk of another terrorist attack occurring was low. However, extra precautions were established to protect racers and families including requiring runners to place their belongings in clear plastic bags provided for them (Matarese, 2013).

Risk Management

Risk management requires agencies to perform actions to prepare for and prevent risk before, during, and after a threat occurs. Agencies use risk assessment and decision-making to create organized and effective prevention and response strategies. Therefore, access to technology, data, and open communication is essential. During the risk management phase, the following questions are asked:

- Once the decisions are communicated to the institutions or individuals responsible to carry them out, is further communication to lower levels required? How is this done? Are protocols designed with that goal?
- Are the specific responsibilities of each level (national, regional, local) established? How?
- Are data gathered about the effective implementation of the measures adopted (monitoring)? How? Who is responsible to do that? Is that information passed on to the authorities? How?
- How is the effectiveness of the measures established? By whom? Is this communicated to higher authorities? How? (Kennedy et al., 2011, p. 35).

Response agencies develop specific mandates, such as the Incident Command System (ICS) created by the United States Federal Emergency Management Agency

(FEMA), to address risks. As described on the FEMA (2013) Web site, the ICS is effective in dealing with all types of hazards and:

- Allows for the integration of facilities, equipment, personnel, procedures and communications operating within a common organization structure.
- Enables a coordinated response among various jurisdictions and functional agencies, both public and private.
- Establishes common processes for planning and managing resources.

By focusing on five "functional areas": Command, Planning, Logistics, Operations, and Finance/Administration, and providing training and resources for each function, agencies can adapt ICS to their needs when facing any type of disaster. ICS can be used for everything from Hurricane Sandy and police activity to mountain travel and rescue courses taught by state ski patrols.

Quick response mitigates harm. When the two bombs exploded at the Boston Marathon, medics responded with lightning speed, thus minimizing the deaths of those who were injured from the bombs. While around 264 people were hurt by the two blasts, all of those rescued alive from the bombings survived (Kotz, 2013). This is attributed to the speed at which medical personnel responded by making their tents into a "mass-casualty triage unit." In addition, backup medical personnel helped rescue injured victims and, in minutes, bring them to eight separate hospitals in Boston. At the hospitals themselves, everyone was on call and ready to perform emergency surgery on all victims (Gawande, 2013). While it can be argued that the risk of a terrorist attack occurring was not properly assessed (since it was not prevented), people were in the right place to act quickly and effectively to mitigate the damage created by the blasts.

Data Needs and Analysis Strategies in the Application of the Common Methodology Approach Applied to Criminology and Counterterrorism

Data Sources and Collection

In studying crime and terrorism, the careful gathering and analyses of data constitute the first steps in the process. Data can be used to build risk models, which allow law enforcement and policy makers to understand better the probability of an event occurring. Data come in many forms, both qualitative and quantitative. In the past, data were collected in mainly three ways: (1) by reports from law enforcement, (2) by victims and witnesses of a crime, and (3) by interviews and statements made by offenders (LaFree, 2012, p. 42). For certain events, such as terrorism and cybercrime, these sources may not give enough information regarding the incident that took place. Terrorist attacks are low frequency and high impact (LFHI), meaning that they do not occur often but when they do happen, they injure or kill many people. The events are shocking, but because they are rare, it is difficult to develop patterns of occurrence, providing clues for future incidents. Thus, as we discussed above, analysts are left to supplement confidential intelligence gathering using open source data including media, online communities, and crowd sourcing to gather information (p. 42). While these strategies allow more information to be collected, they also raise issues regarding the validity and legitimacy of these data sources.

Recently, through increased access to the Internet and data centers, the amount of available information has vastly increased. Crime statistics, data obtained through surveys and questionnaires, information collected on people's backgrounds and criminal history, surveillance, eyewitness reports, and maps all can be used to ascertain the nature of a threat, the likelihood of an event occurring, and the damage that the threat could create if it happened. The difficulties in connecting these risk factors to actual behavior, however, confound law enforcement and present new dilemmas in managing, analyzing, and applying data analysis in decision-making, including issues related to privacy.

In the UK, for example, surveillance collected through closed-circuit television (CCTV) has been promoted as an important crime prevention tool in specific locations (Van Brunschot & Kennedy, 2011, p. 10). If a crime is committed in front of a camera, the video footage can be used as data for identifying the suspect(s) of the crime (p. 11). In the US, CCTV has been used increasingly in high-risk areas, including street corners prone to drug dealing. In the Boston bombings, a Lord and Taylor security camera picked up the Tsarnaev brothers walking away from the bleachers where they placed the bombs (WCVB, 2013). While this technology proves more effective in providing data for solving crimes after something occurs rather than deterring the crime in the first place, in the case of the Boston bombings, it gave qualitative information regarding terrorists who were yet to be identified and who could likely act again.

Recently, law enforcement used online communities including Twitter, Facebook, and Reddit to gather data, as well as to communicate with the public during crises. However, information gained through these interfaces must be approached with caution. For example, when the police released a low quality photo of one of the Boston bombing suspects, civilians took it upon themselves to determine the identity of the suspect. Through the Web site Reddit, an open-source community-based Web page that allows people to create groups to discuss any topic, users began uploading both accurate and inaccurate information regarding the bombings in an attempt to identify and find the suspects. The lack of a filter, however, encouraged the online mob to go after an innocent man, who had been missing since March. His family came under attack from false accusations.

During the arrest of the younger brother in the bombing, Dzhokhar, 272,000 users were reading the Reddit page related to the bombings. According to *Time* magazine, this is close to the number of people watching the larger news agencies (Pickert & Sorenson, 2013). Such a powerful Web site is extremely useful in connecting individuals, but can also have dangerous consequences if the information given is misleading and not properly vetted by authorities.

Surowiecki (2013) argues that the problems of misidentification encountered in Boston can be controlled if crowd-sourcing sites are given the same data (or in the case of the Boston bombings proper photographs or images of the suspects) as officials with some careful instruction on what is known and not known about the circumstances of the case. "Reddit had no real chance of identifying the right suspects because it didn't have access to the information that mattered" (Surowiecki, 2013). Surowiecki offers suggestions as to how a site like Reddit could be reformatted to allow the public to give better information including posting pictures without comments (so that readers can make their own opinions) and using a voting system to determine which photos and evidence should be passed to authorities. Surowiecki points to the positive results from the National Aeronautics and Space Administration's (NASA) Clickworkers Web site that lets people look at photos of Mars and classify them as a crowd-source application. However, as Surowiecki points out, having a controlled Web site would significantly decrease traffic since the public uses Reddit not only to solve the problem but also to openly interject in controversies, get gossip, and talk with others.

Beyond a focus on offenders, computational strategies that focus on risk factors in locations offer new opportunities for risk assessment. For example, Risk Terrain Modeling or RTM is an approach to spatial risk analysis that utilizes a geographic information system (GIS) to attribute qualities of the real world to places on a digitized map. It operationalizes the spatial influence of risk factors to common geographic units, then combines separate layers to produce "risk terrain" maps showing the presence, absence, or intensity of all risk factors at every location throughout the landscape. Theoretically, empirically grounded risk terrain maps show where conditions are conducive for future crimes or other hazardous events to occur. RTM offers a statistically valid way to articulate and communicate criminogenic and vulnerable areas at the micro-level (Caplan & Kennedy, 2011).[3]

This approach is location specific and provides the opportunity to anticipate the contexts in which certain types of crime or terrorism might occur. For example, a study by Rusnak, Kennedy, Eldivan, and Caplan (2012) in Turkey identified the important public buildings and location of mosques as risk indicators that, when clustered, were targets for terrorist attacks. An approach that identifies the contexts in which these events occur, especially for low occurring crimes, allows us to anticipate where risk is highest and to take appropriate precautions.

There are other approaches to data analysis that are based less on analytical strategies and more on how to use alternative data sets in unconventional ways. One such approach has been adopted by the United Nations. The Global Pulse program was created in 2009 by the Executive Office of the United Nations Secretary-General:

> in response to the need for more timely information to track and monitor the impacts of global and local socio-economic crises. The Global Pulse initiative is exploring how new,

[3] Visit www.rutgerscps.org for more information regarding RTM as well as online resources and tutorials on how to use RTM on ARC GIS.

> digital data sources and real-time analytics technologies can help policymakers understand human well-being and emerging vulnerabilities in real-time, in order to better protect populations from shocks (United Nations, 2013).[4]

The program works to investigate "the viability of using new and alternative data sources to support development goals" (United Nations, 2013). Global Pulse gathers information from four sources: (1) online sources including news Web sites, online communities, and e-commerce; (2) the private sector including hotlines, searches, and telecommunications companies; (3) sensors including satellite imagery and video; and (4) crowd sources including information submitted through surveys, maps, etc. Its goal is to harness "big data," or large quantities of data that are difficult to handle, for "monitoring development progress, emerging vulnerabilities and overall population well being" (United Nations, 2013). By exploring and perfecting the processing and analysis of big data, Global Pulse hopes to partner with public and private organizations to create analytical tools that can be formed into policy. Through their "pulse labs," they hope to connect UN Member States to explore methodologies and tools.

Arising Issues Related to Data Collection, Sharing, and Analysis

There are barriers related to the collection and analysis of data. Due to a lack of resources and/or technology, data may not be collected properly or at all. If data are collected, the information may not be reliable as it comes from multiple sources with different interpretations and/or agendas. Data accessibility is also, at times, limited due to the haphazard way in which information is gathered and presented. As mentioned earlier, further difficulty arises when data are deemed by law enforcement to be top secret or only available on a need to know basis. This creates issues of limited access and restricted use especially when global crime affects multiple jurisdictions on a global and local scale.

To improve the quality and accessibility of data, scholars proposed standards for the collection and dissemination of information (Gerring, 2001, 2010; Lieberman, 2010; Sheehan, 2012). This "criteria framework" has been offered for both small and large sample sizes, as well as both qualitative and quantitative data (Sheehan, 2012, p. 14). In reviewing multiple terrorism data sets available online, Sheehan cites Schmid (2004) and describes how it is necessary for data to be questioned and scrutinized to meet academic and statistical standards. During his review of these databases, Sheehan found that there were many discrepancies across them:

> since much of the data is derived from media sources in real time, and since its developers have frequently used different definitions and coding rules, no one dataset is completely comprehensive or exhaustive and there is a great deal of variability across datasets (p. 15).

Some further issues that arise include the varied definitions of terrorism; the lack of transparency of information; the validity and reliability of information; and the

[4] Go to www.unglobalpulse.org to see more information about Global Pulse.

way in which it is collected (p. 19). To mitigate such issues, Sheehan proposes the following criteria for evaluating terrorism databases:

- Conceptual clarity: Is the definition of terrorism used in construction of the database specified?
- Context and immediacy of observations: Do the authors report the context and immediacy of the observations?
- Citation transparency: Are the actual sources of the data described? Are clear references to original data provided?
- Coding consistency: Do the authors provide a codebook? Do they discuss how they resolved coding conflicts and make decisions in ambiguous cases?
- Certainty: Are contradictory facts reported?
- Conflict of interest issues: Are funding sources and other potential conflicts of interest reported?
- Convenience/functionality: How accessible is the database? Can it be downloaded? Can it be disaggregated for fine analyses? (drawn from Table 2, p. 21)

These criteria can be generalized for all types of crime databases including cybercrime, human trafficking, drug trafficking, weapons trafficking, and many others. Further, these principles can be used before data are collected to create a structure by which information is gathered appropriately. If government agencies and law enforcement understand what their data should look like, they can create policy that outlines the methods by which they should be collected and shared.

Intelligence sharing between law enforcement agencies is critical in preventing terrorism (and other crimes). The 9/11 Commission reported that the lack of intelligence sharing was one of the leading reasons why the attacks were not prevented (National Commission on Terrorist Attacks Upon the United States, 2004). In response, the US created state-run "fusion centers." These centers allow for the collaboration of intelligence gathering and sharing between multiple law enforcement agencies (Carter & Chermak, 2012, p. 65). This type of program was first used in the 1980s when "regional intelligence centers" were created to share information regarding drug incidents. The High Intensity Drug Trafficking Area (HIDTA) created a space for local, state, and national law enforcement to share intelligence regarding drug trafficking. In the 1990s, the US Bureau of Alcohol, Tobacco, Firearms, and Explosives formed Crime Gun Centers. They analyzed data regarding gun trafficking and also worked with HIDTA to identify drug dealers who were using illegal weapons (Carter & Carter, 2009, p. 1324).

Post 9/11, fusion centers were expanded and federally funded with the intent that all law enforcement agencies have access to data collected by the intelligence community, including classified information, in a more seamless manner (p. 1325). Furthermore, local fusion centers recruited qualified federal employees and federal funding became more available for operations. Training was provided to fusion centers to help them develop and become more sustainable (p. 1326). However, critics wonder if these fusion centers can actually be sustainable, given that federal funding is not permanent; it is an enormous task to train law enforcement across the country to work effectively with these centers, and the collection of data in certain cases raises issues regarding civil liberties and human rights (pp. 1325–1326).

There is a further problem:

> Intelligence leaders and analysts ... have provided anecdotal support for the conclusion that there are significant limits to both the amount and quality of information shared and have voiced frustrations about the inability to accurately assess performance (Carter & Chermak, 2012, p. 73).

This issue, Carter and Chermak argue, is not related to a lack of information but to the inability to process and organize the large quantity of data received at the fusion centers (p. 73). Specifically, fusion centers are yet to perfect translational skills, in which researchers take collected data, analyze them, and make recommendations and predictions as to where the threats exist. Carter and Chermak argue that these holes can be filled through increased partnership with academics who are trained in statistical data analysis (p. 86) but the institutional barriers to sharing classified data would have to be overcome before this becomes a reality. Throughout the three phases of the common methodology (risk assessment, decision-making, and risk management), data are continuously collected, organized, and analyzed to create recommendations regarding the prevention of and response to hazards. In section "Common Methodology in Support of Global Translational Perspectives: Terrorism and Cybercrime," when examining case studies related to the Istanbul bombings of 2003 and the Stuxnet computer virus, we, once again, explore how data and intelligence, and the issues that accompany their collection and analysis, affect the ability of law enforcement to deal with incidents of global crime.

We can begin, in looking at the case studies of terrorism and cybercrime, by first providing some background information regarding each threat. We will show how "common methodology" (risk assessment, decision-making, and risk management), discussed above, can be used to address these crimes at the global and local levels. In both cases studies, we address the barriers to effective prevention that include lack of data, lack of communication and cooperation, lack of technology, and lack of other resources.

Part III. Common Methodology in Support of Global Translational Perspectives: Terrorism and Cybercrime

We can begin, in looking at the case studies of terrorism and cybercrime, by first providing some background information regarding each threat. We will show how "common methodology" (risk assessment, decision-making, and risk management), discussed above, can be used to address these crimes at the global and local levels. In both cases studies, we address the barriers to effective prevention that include lack of data, lack of communication and cooperation, lack of technology, and lack of other resources.

Terrorism

Background

This section examines the local and global aspects of terrorism, first by demonstrating how crime fuels terrorism. We will then summarize the policy decisions and legal actions that have been taken to protect nations from further terrorist onslaughts. While some of these attempts have been successful at deterring terrorist activities, or criminal activities that support terrorism, ongoing issues appear with regard to human rights that arise through profiling by race, religion, or ethnicity. We then examine how risk analysis can be used through the use of a common methodology (risk assessment, decision-making, and risk management) to prevent, prepare for, mitigate, and respond to acts of terrorism. We specifically use the case of the 2003 terrorist bombings in Turkey to analyze what law enforcement did and continues to do to deal with the threat of terrorism.

Stage 1: Risk Assessment and the Crime Terror Continuum

The link between crime and terrorism was not firmly established until recently (Perri, Lichtenwald, & MacKenzie, 2009). Following the attacks of 9/11, the United Nations Security Council (UNSC) adopted a resolution which noted a "... close connection between international terrorism and transnational organized crime, illicit drugs, money laundering, illegal arms-trafficking, and illegal movement of nuclear, chemical, biological and other potentially deadly materials" (UNSC, 2001, p. 3). Recently, Yury Fedotov, the Executive Director of the UN Office on Drugs and Crime (UNODC), referred to the double-edged nature of globalization, as we discussed earlier. He explained how open borders, open markets, and ease of travel and communication have profited both terrorists and criminals by forming a link between loose networks. These networks allow criminals to pool their resources and expertise to increase their capacity to do harm at the local level through global means (UN News Centre, 2011).

At the same time, the forces of globalization have limited terrorists with regard to their own finances. Especially in the post 9/11 era, with the increased "Global War on Terror," many terrorist groups have been pressured to find alternative financial and material support beyond contributions by sympathetic members and supporting states. Close monitoring is a factor pushing the transnational terrorist networks to be more dependent on criminal activity (Dishman, 2001; Hutchinson & O'Malley, 2007). Following the UNSC's resolution no.1373, the G8 Recommendations on Transnational Crime have also drawn attention to the:

> … problem of terrorist organizations supporting their activities through the commission of other crimes and recommended that States strengthen their response to the interaction between international terrorism and organized criminal activities, in particular money laundering, illegal drug trafficking, use of illegal migration networks and illegal trafficking in firearms (Dandurand & Chin, 2004, p. 2).

According to a detailed analysis of the reports of the United Nations Member States and results of a questionnaire that was sent through official channels to Member States by Dandurand and Chin (2004), there are at least three ways in which terrorist networks are judged to become involved in criminal activity. First, the criminal activities that are related to terrorism include gathering information on the behalf of terrorists, laundering money to fund terrorist activities, providing communication support, and helping with logistics of terrorist attacks (p. 4). Accordingly, most of the activities in which terrorist groups become involved in pursuit of their operations are already crimes. Second, driven by the need for financial support, terrorist groups participate in profitable crimes (e.g., trafficking and smuggling in drugs and humans) to finance their activities. Third, if weapons, tools, and facilitating conditions are not available, terrorist groups become immersed in different conventional and emerging crimes (arms trafficking, smuggling of nuclear, biological, and other hazardous material, cybercrime, identity theft, petty theft, etc.) to provide these means.

Several guerrilla groups have established relationships with crime groups and/or engage in criminal activities. In the most notorious example during the Kosovo conflict, it was reported that the Kosovo Liberation Army (KLA) trafficked heroin to raise money for its operations. The Revolutionary Armed Forces of Colombia (FARC) has continuously drawn its revenue from narcotics and has been labeled as a narco-terror group involved in kidnapping, extortion, and drug trafficking. Further evidence also indicates that terrorist groups in Spain, Sri Lanka, Turkey, and Lebanon engage in drug trafficking and other crimes to finance their operations (Dishman, 2001, p. 43).

In the responses to the United Nations questionnaire, terrorist groups worldwide were reported to be involved in organized crime. Many countries suggested that these groups were involved in illegal drug trade, arms trafficking, theft of firearms and explosives, corruption and attempts to corrupt public officials, smuggling of illegal migrants, falsification of travel and other official documents, money laundering, and illegal trafficking in chemical materials. In addition, countries reported an increased link between crime and terrorism suggesting that the political ideology of terrorist groups is replaced by profit and greed as the main motivation for operations (p. 24).

The link of terrorists to crime shown through this extensive analysis of cross-national data has nudged countries to face the implications of such a continuum. On the international level, especially after 9/11, efforts were made to disrupt the crime–terrorism continuum. Nonetheless, as Dandurand and Chin (2004) state:

> ... the international criminal justice cooperation regime is still at its very early stages of development. It is still confronted with persistent difficulties resulting from inconsistencies among the international agreements that have evolved to support it as well as from the lack of harmony and compatibility between national justice systems (p. 32).

Despite this state of vagueness and disharmony, the link between various forms of crime and terrorism might be used as the starting point to target terrorism: "... some of the most effective instruments governments have at their disposal to combat terrorism are their law enforcement and criminal justice system" (p. 32). A key element in the study of the crime terror continuum is the nature of the organizations that support or facilitate terror. There has been a great deal of interest in the narco-terrorists who use drug crime to control political agendas in South America and Asia. Narco-terrorists commit crimes to support their participation in the drug trade and commit terrorist acts to destabilize governments. Until recently, it was believed that terrorist organizations did not often demonstrate this duality of purpose. They may involve themselves in crime but only for the purpose of facilitating their political agendas. However, research by Curtis and Karacan suggests that this pattern is changing as terrorists become more closely entwined with criminal groups through the exchange of commodities such as drugs for arms (Curtis & Karacan, 2002). There is even increasing evidence to suggest the phenomenon of "fighters turned felons" that appears as these groups become heavily involved in crime to finance their activities (p. 4).

This approach to the crime terrorism continuum does not deny the importance of identifying activity that, in and of itself, ties to the ideology of the groups and the indoctrination of members. It is important to understand that the tracking of extremists can be facilitated in this way. However, monitoring them falls outside of the expertise of most law enforcement agencies. Even some specialists tasked to follow these organizations are confronted with language and cultural barriers, making the task of identifying patterns difficult. This ideological structure, however, can be detected through the relationships that local law enforcement establishes with the community in which terrorist groups operate, a point that we will turn to momentarily.

A number of questions are raised about the extent to which criminal activity will reveal the potential threat of terror. While the more organized terror groups such as the Irish Republican Army (IRA), the Kurdistan Workers' Party (PKK), and the Basque Homeland and Freedom (ETA) have a broad public image, most transnational terror groups operating in local environments maintain the goal of remaining invisible, undetected by law enforcement, until the opportunity to strike appears. Therefore, there is a daunting challenge for law enforcement to manage terror threats when the terrorist may be an otherwise law-abiding citizen whose first crime is the act of terror. This was the case of the London bombers who attacked buses and subway stations in 2005. They had no previous criminal records.

However, there is also a serious challenge to these groups to be able to mobilize resources with which to engage in terrorist activities. They often need to break the law and operate on the margins to support their initiatives. They launder money. They obtain false identities and recruit new members. They move people into locations that assist the attacks (sometimes breaking immigration laws) and conduct surveillance against their intended targets. It is in this area of operational support, through what is referred to as "enterprise crime," that we can establish our first point of understanding of how the crime terror continuum may operate as an ongoing illegal business for the terrorist group.

Enterprise crime is the "sale of illegal goods and services to customers who know that the goods or services are illegal" (Haller, 1990, p. 207). The sale of banned drugs or pornography, the operation of unlicensed gambling houses, loan sharking, and "contract killing" are all examples of enterprise crime. So, too, are arms smuggling, identity theft, and trafficking in human beings (Sacco & Kennedy, 2010, p. 344). The elements of the crime are rationally ordered and directed towards the pursuit of profit (Gottschalk, 2009). It is the economic component, rather than the motivation of the offender, that gives this kind of crime its distinct character (Bouchard & Wilkins, 2009).

What can we learn about how enterprise crime groups function that would help us understand terror groups? What patterns appear in these operations that are necessary in any enterprise to bring about success? Also, in prevention, what have been the most effective ways to curtail enterprise crime, for example, drug cartels and gambling syndicates? What are the links between these enterprise crimes and terror groups? How much does one rely on the other? Finally, at what point do terror groups morph into enterprise crime operations and does this make them more or less difficult to detect and deter?

An advantage of looking at terrorism from an enterprise crime point of view is that it allows us to use existing models of interagency policing. As an example, it is not in the interest of the terrorist to be detected by local law enforcement. In fact, as we saw in the bombings in Britain, it is unlikely that this will occur, as most of the terrorists would have legal documents and would be encouraged not to break the law. However, in their efforts to compile the instruments of mass destruction to facilitate their actions, they have to operate in a coordinated enterprise that makes them vulnerable to detection through other means.

Accordingly, the acknowledged link between crime and terror on the global scale can translate into a counter-terrorism policy formulated by local governments, law enforcement, and criminal justice systems that focuses on local crime. Still, the reader is cautioned against the real-life implications of the focus on the crime and terrorism continuum and the trade-offs between securitization and civil liberties. From an enforcement perspective, especially in the case of targeting emergent crimes such as smuggling of persons and cybercrime at a local scale, the traditional approach to enforcing criminal law might be insufficient, as these crimes are clandestine in nature (i.e., the difficulty in identifying the victims, offenders, and crime locations). Furthermore, even if the characteristics of the crime and the mechanisms leading to it are identified, unlike conventional violent and property crime response, the responsibility to react to such mechanisms cannot be solely imposed on local authorities.

Stage 2: Decision-Making, Current Practice, and Legal Considerations in Regards to Combating Terrorism

There are very significant constitutional, legal, and operational considerations that enter the discussion about national/local cooperation in this area. The basic structure of American federalism seeks to keep the national and state spheres separate, and there are strict legal criteria for determining when and how these barriers may be breached. In addition to the legal barriers, operational decisions have been made within the FBI, for example, to keep separate the criminal investigative (directed to prosecution) and the intelligence gathering activities and information, (directed to prevention) so as not to legally jeopardize the success of either activity. These issues are not merely a matter of refusing to cooperate or to share information, although that certainly also enters the picture, and must inform any discussion of jurisdiction.

While the US government is interested in the societal context and motivation of foreign grown terrorism that may be aimed at the population of the country, these are conventionally seen as foreign policy issues. The New York Police Department may be justified in creating bureaus in London and Jerusalem to share expertise with their fellow counterterrorist experts there and to get early warning where possible. There seems to be little justification, however, for local police departments in small towns and cities across the country to embark on major local terrorism intelligence gathering projects. While local law enforcement in Idaho should indeed be collecting good intelligence on the boys with guns in the hills, including their connections to drug running and other crimes, the threat from Al Qaeda appears distant (Anarumo, 2011). All these, then, suggest a grid outlining boundaries between primarily local and international threats/risks, with attendant links to appropriate national and local government security agencies.

Would scanning activities that might be designated "precursor to terrorism" crimes, give us clues in identifying terror groups about to attack? Had officials detected that some of the terrorists of 9/11 had expired visas, they may have prevented them from being present during the attack.

Can we develop a pattern from individual acts or is it more effective to look for organized activities? This would lead us to groups that, through enterprise activities (both inside and outside of criminal actions), obtain the wherewithal to launch an attack. The value of increased attention on organizational activities forces a group to adapt its target lists. Such changes increase the likelihood of detection.

If we look at the connection of enterprise crime to terror, the enforcement role is less directed towards the compilation of minor crimes in a pattern of terror threat than to a coordinated local stream of intelligence about the enterprise activities of groups within communities and the threats that they pose. As has been the case in efforts to curtail juvenile gangs, an effective role of law enforcement has been to partner with the communities as eyes and ears to provide local intelligence. Understanding the ways in which local crime groups form, how they choose their targets and opportunities, and what motivates them have proven to be efficient ways for law enforcement to influence the actions of these groups. Even though the terrorist threat is particularly dangerous, the warning signs that come from the actions of these groups, including criminal activity, can be identified within the communities in which these groups function.

A particular dilemma that develops in targeting these crime groups is that they often are seen as supportive of the communities' more general aims. Their threats are not directed against the local community but rather at governments or people somewhere else who are seen as opponents to the community. Even worse, in the efforts to detect and remove dangerous elements in these neighborhoods, the police often develop strained relationships with local leaders who feel that law enforcement is not sympathetic to their religion or values. In the aftermath of the London subway bombings and of the discovery of a subsequent plot to blow up planes, the police pushed hard, with mixed results, to call on the Muslim communities to develop means by which they can work in a cooperative fashion to detect and deter further threats.

This work is difficult as the local leadership needs to be able to promote the view that it is representing the needs of its constituents under threat from others while making it clear that they will support the law and help in the removal of dangerous individuals amongst them. The complications of religion and culture become an important consideration in these types of community relations and have a direct effect on the way police enlist civilian support in crime suppression.

Again, the parallels to common crime also exist in the role that terror groups or supporting agencies play in intimidating local communities. It is not uncommon for criminal enterprise groups to use protection rackets to control people within ethnic groups, either extorting resources or silence through the threat of violence (Sacco & Kennedy, 2010). How extensive this type of activity is in locations that may spawn insipient terror groups is not clear, although there is evidence for this type of tactic in both the Loyalist and Republican areas of Northern Ireland, for example. In parallel to the local gangs, threats from terror groups can include direct action against individuals or threats against witnesses or informants who provide information about gang activities.

Government responses often make this type of cooperation difficult. When analyzing the effects of the legislation that was enacted post 9/11 by the Bush administration, scholars have argued (Brané & Lundholm, 2008; Cohen, 2010; Cole, 2003) that such policies adversely affected the noncitizens living in the US, most of whom had no relation to the crimes committed on the World Trade Center. Furthermore, as Cohen argues, these laws counteract the basis for the foundation of the Equal Protection Clause of the Fourteenth Amendment. As Cohen (2010) states:

> The terrorist attacks engendered a perception of vulnerability, which understandably spurred broadly sweeping legislation aimed at protecting the country from further harm. However, worthy their aims, though, running throughout many of the new policies that the United States adopted in the wake of 9/11 was a systematic differentiation between American citizens and aliens that appears to be unbounded by any concern for the aliens' constitutional right of equal protection under the laws (p. 1332).

Immigration policy is predominately focused on securing borders and keeping people out, which can have adverse effects on those who are either brought or forced to enter the country illegally. In the case of post 9/11, profiling has increasingly become a means of determining who could be a suspected terrorist. Since the attacks on the World Trade Center were organized by a radical Muslim terrorist group, Muslims living in the US, both citizens and noncitizens, have been targeted by the public, the media, and policy alike. This was the case with the scrutiny over President Obama's religion when he was running for President in 2009. In addition, people who weren't Muslim but who "looked" as if they were from the Middle East suffered scrutiny and mistrust from other ethnic groups, as well as the government and law enforcement. Heightened airport security has also used profiling to detain travelers for questioning. The pressure to stay ahead of the threats posed by the unseen terrorist has made it difficult for political leaders to turn back terror laws, even in face of evidence that they have exceeded the bounds of what was previously seen as impinging on peoples' rights (Merola, 2012).

On a local basis, illegal immigrants and "suspected" terrorists have been detained in local jails, in many cases without any ability to seek counsel or family. Following the attacks of 9/11, the Immigration and Naturalization Service (INS) and the Department of Justice imprisoned noncitizens, calling it "mass preventive detention." The detainees were imprisoned under immigration law and thus would not be granted the same rights as detained citizens (Cole, 2003 as cited in Brané & Lundholm, 2008). The US Immigration and Customs Enforcement's (ICE) Detention and Removal Operations (DRO) increased their budget 104 % from 2005 to 2009 (TRAC, 2010). As stated by the Transactional Records Access Clearinghouse (TRAC) (2010):

> The significant increases in funding provided by Congress were made with the promise that ICE would give priority to detaining and removing aliens who were widely believed to pose a real threat to the safety of the United States. Especially to be targeted were non-citizens in our midst who had been convicted of a crime regardless of whether they entered the country legally or illegally, whether they were long-time legal permanent residents ("green-card holder") or short-term temporary workers, visitors with proper authorization, or aliens who had been working or staying illegally in this country.

As described by Brané and Lundholm (2008), the legality of US actions which have taken place through "mass preventive detention" can be challenged through certain articles in the Refugee Convention, "which does not encourage the kind of widespread practice of detention as a deterrent that exists in the US" (p. 156). The International Covenant on Civil and Political Rights (ICCPR), states that "... no-one shall be subjected to arbitrary arrest or detention" (p. 156) and that people should have "the right to recognition as a person before the law and equality before the law and equal protection of the law" (p. 158) among other articles. The US has ratified both the Refugee Convention and the ICCPR. However, the fear of the outsider continues to influence the debate about readiness to deal with terrorism threats in the country.

The "War on Terror" spurred by the US post 9/11 also influenced other countries to pass antiterrorist legislation. However, unlike the US, the European Court of Human Rights (ECHR) has ruled that "… neither rendition nor other removal of suspected terrorists are allowed absent guaranteed protections of their human rights" (Aronofsky & Cooper, 2009, p. 601). Furthermore, the Turkish government found that the presence of military influence, whether through military courts or military judges, questions the legitimacy and efficacy of sentencing. The ECHR also requires that crimes committed by government officials including murder and torture be fully investigated (p. 602).

In terms of the treatment of detainees in prison, the ECHR states that all assaults on prisoners be fully investigated (p. 605). Furthermore, the UK will not use evidence obtained through torture in court (p. 608). In terms of the right for privacy and general human rights, the UK will not allow illegal surveillance (p. 611). The ECHR requires that victims of human rights abuses are entitled to legal proceedings (p. 609).

The most recent rulings by the current US administration sought to restore some of the rights removed during the post 9/11 reactions. As pointed out above, these include a ban on torture. However, the Obama administration was not able to find a way to bring terror defendants to the US for trial and close the Guantanamo Bay Prison. In addition, after much deliberation, it decided not to pursue charges against CIA employees who were accused of torturing captured combatants. These controversial decisions put the US government in a difficult place concerning the balance of aggressive pursuit of terrorist suspects while protecting their rights when captured.

Stage 3: Risk Management

As explained in detail earlier, the "crime" portion of the crime–terrorism continuum generally refers to a number of possibilities: finance terrorist activities through criminal ventures; such as drug or human trafficking; collaboration between terrorist and criminal gangs for protection; and supply of equipment and materials and special skills and services. There is also a "precursor crime" notion which holds that there will be ordinary illegal activities leading to a terrorist act which can be spotted by local law enforcement and perhaps prevent the act. If these are valid distinctions, we may need to approach the possible crime–terrorism continuum, and the related national–local collaboration possibilities, very differently for these varieties of terrorism. Staying with 9/11 as an example, useful intelligence would be gathered overseas by national security agencies and through cooperation with foreign agencies.

While elements of national terror groups become a part of the transnational threat, the current Islamic terror appears to thrive across borders, supported by the modern communications of the Internet and the globalization of modern economies, including the rapid movement of people and money. In this climate, we have the emergence, as well, of national representatives of these global movements tied together by religious fanaticism. This is set into a context of a world that is highly dependent on all of these global factors to function, as we pointed out in the first chapter, including the tightly woven supply chains for goods and services that, if disrupted, can easily destabilize major economies. Thus, the features of modern life that allows for easy movement across borders and around the world become the same features that crime syndicates and global terror groups are able to exploit.

The important insights provided by the research on the major terror groups of the 1980s and the 1990s show how closely intertwined they became with international drug cartels and international arms smugglers (Björnehed, 2004). The need for cash to pay for guns led the IRA to trade expertise in tactics to South American narco-terrorists who paid in drugs. In turn, the IRA sold the drugs and bought guns. When the training money ran out, the IRA robbed banks to pay for guns but then it just started to rob banks for the money—a classic fighter to felon phenomenon.

Importantly, the ability to move goods and arms requires a great deal of support from government agencies operating in unstable countries, where officials can be easily suborned to allow goods to pass undetected. The need for weapons is reinforced particularly in the national terror groups, which still resort to armed action against police and the army (as in the Kurdistan Workers Party or the PKK). The standard form of attack by international terrorists is still bombing, which requires substantial technical expertise and supplies.

In this delicate balance, there is a need to protect targets and remove opportunities for aggression. This appears a daunting task as subways and airplanes appear easy prey. However, despite the repeated onslaughts, the patterns of behavior have been fairly similar, with mobile attackers carrying bombs. Even the apparent simplicity of these types of attacks creates demanding organizational strains on these groups. Recruitment in itself is a risky activity requiring secrecy and capital. Terrorists must also obtain materials for making bombs, conduct surveillance on their targets, and initiate their attack without being flagged. At any one of these steps, there is danger of detection. With increased surveillance, target hardening, and proactive supervision, carrying out destructive measures becomes more difficult.

Most target hardening that occurs comes as a direct result of responding to crime problems, not fear of terrorism, thus strengthening the relationship between crime and terror. Originally, concerns about social disorder spurred the implementation of CCTV across North America and in the UK. Cameras were only later thought of as a way of also monitoring and deterring the IRA bombing threat. Understanding this provides further support for the notion that terrorists must resort to similar strategies that criminals follow to remain undetected and undeterred. Despite the view that suicide bombers cannot be stopped as they don't care about their own safety, if the target is too secure, they may be deterred from launching the attack in the first place.

Any assessments of target hardening need to consider how much terrorism has been influenced by crime reduction strategies (Newman & Clarke, 2003). If we are convinced that crime has gone down, as a consequence, terrorism that relies on the delivery of bombs to targets should be equally influenced. However, we are at a bit of a loss about the true effectiveness of these programs as little research has been done on any one of these approaches. As pointed out in a review for the Campbell Collaborative Criminal Justice Consortium, little or no systematic evaluations of counterterrorism strategies (with the exception of metal detectors at airports) have been conducted (Lum, Kennedy, & Sherley, 2006). The experience with crime prevention assessment has been much more robust and we have much to learn from assessments of community-based crime prevention programs, community policing, intelligence led policing, and environmental target hardening strategies that have appeared in the research literature (see the Web page of the Campbell Collaborative, 2013). If the parallels are as we say, these approaches provide important models for us to adopt in understanding and managing terror threats. In the next section we focus on a case study, the 2003 Istanbul bombings, to show how common methodology can be used to analyze risk and respond to emerging threats.

Case Study: Risk Analysis of Terrorist Bombings in Istanbul Using Common Methodology

To Islamist extremists, and the Al Qaeda organization specifically, any country that does not follow *Salafism*, an ideology that follows the scriptural interpretation of the Quran, is misguided.

> The participants of this global jihadist network share, to some extent, a vision of the world. According to this vision, the world has decayed into a morass of greed and moral depravity. They blame western influence and corrupt governments of Muslim countries for corrupting their religion (Ozkan, 2013, p. 29).

Although most people who follow *Salafism* hope to change society by peaceful means, there is a small and dangerous group which believes that the only way to return the world to what it was before western influence is to perform acts of violence (p. 30). Since extremist groups had limited success at overthrowing their own governments, terrorists now target Western countries and Western interests in Middle Eastern nations.

Turkey is a secular country. Formed into a Republic in 1923 by Mustafa Kemal, called Atatürk (Father of the Turks), the first government of Turkey imposed a Turkish identity where a person's rights came second to the state (Senay, 2008, p. 964). After the fall of the Ottoman Empire, the Turkish Republic wanted to create its own identity, to distinguish it from Ottoman or Arabic influence (Voloder, 2012, p. 841). The Kemalist principles pushed for a homogenous Turkey, one language (Turkish), one ethnic group (Turkish), one religion (Islam) and one interpretation of Islam. However, Atatürk also promoted Western government (a Parliamentary system), policies (the separation of church and state), and culture predominantly void of Islamic images or dress. Further antireligious policies included banning private Islamic schools, restricting the calls to prayers used by imams to only be recited in Turkish;

only publishing one interpretation of the Quran; and forbidding headscarves in government offices and public institutions (Ozkan, 2013, p. 169). Shively (2008) describes the reasoning behind these Turkish laws:

> The idea is that religion should not be in the hands of a powerful and independent cleric elite (*ulema*) that can rival government power, but should be brought under the control of the non-religious state, where it no longer poses a potential threat to government hegemony ... the Turkish state promotes the notion that Islam can be separated out from other types of social activities, including politics, to create a neutral, non-religious, public space and institutions (pp. 684–685).[5]

Therefore, Islam is regulated and controlled under the Directorate of Religious Affairs (p. 684).

In 1945, the Democrat Party won the national election and worked to revive Islamic traditions (Senay, 2008, p. 965). In 1950, laws were created that allowed Arabic to be used in prayers. The enforcement of an immigration policy between Greece and Turkey in which Christians moved to Greece and Muslims moved to Turkey increased the number of Turks in the country who followed Islam (Doğruel & Leman, 2009, p. 603). This was followed by the 1961 Constitution that expanded human and civil rights allowing for more liberal citizenship requirements (Senay, 2008, p. 965). However, in 1982, after the military coup which took over the government in 1980, many of the civil liberties granted under the 1961 Constitution were restricted, including rights for the Kurdish minority who were not distinguished from the Turks (p. 965).

Ninety-nine per cent of the Turkish population is Muslim. In 2008, between 70 and 75 % of citizens were Turkish, 18 % were Kurdish, and 7–12 % were other minorities (CIA, 2013). However, secular policies created a place for more conservatively religious people to want to battle the "oppressors," in this case the Turkish government and the Western interests within Turkey (Ozkan, 2013, p. 168). This fueled radical Islamists to create a terrorist organization within Turkey, including Hizbullah and more recently, Al Qaeda Turkey (AQT). These cells were formed by Turkish jihadists (p. 146) who declared that Turkey is a *Dar al-Harb*, or a country with which Muslims are at war (p. 153). Interestingly, the recent events in Turkey have pitted secular forces against a conservatively religious government.

Islamic extremism has existed in Turkey since the 1979 Iranian revolt in which the Iranian government was overthrown and replaced by the religious elite (p. 195). Following Iran's example, through the organization Hizbullah, many Turkish extremists believed they could take over their own government in the same fashion. Members of Hizbullah traveled to Iran to be trained and, upon returning to Turkey, hoped to change government leadership through diplomatic means. However, after the 1980 military coup, Hizbullah changed tactics and took arms against the State, killing many over the course of twenty years (p. 195). On January 17, 2000, the Turkish National Police killed Huseyin Velioglu, the leader of Hizbullah and gathered intelligence about other members through captured archives. Using this information, law enforcement stopped all Hizbullah activity by the end of 2000 (p. 196).

---

[5] Cited from Davison (2003, p. 341) and White (2002, p. 4).

Ozkan states that it took the police twenty years to find Velioglu because they were distracted by their efforts to stop the PKK, a violent Marxist–Leninist group operating in Southern Turkey (p. 197). He states that the law enforcement's preoccupation with the PKK allowed Hizbullah to grow and to organize. In addition, it was able to recruit and train future jihadi, many of whom later joined the AQT, the group responsible for the Istanbul bombings in November 2003 (p. 197).

The AQT was led by Habib Aktas, who returned to Turkey in 2002 after being trained in an Afghanistan jihad camp (p. 146). Aktas and his followers were able to get funding, received in small transfers to multiple accounts, from Al Qaeda in Iran, for their attacks (p. 160). Aktas then created a detergent company called *Gokkusagi* as a cover to make explosives (p. 148). With the help of his team, he was able to produce 5,181 pounds of bomb materials in one month that he installed in four separate trucks, all of which carried the *Gokkusagi* logo. The bombs were electronically connected to a switch on the trucks' dashboards allowing the suicide bomber to trigger the bombs at the right time (p. 149). After some reconnaissance, the original targets, the American and Israeli consulates, were found to be too well protected and would not create mass casualties if bombed (p. 147). In the end, the group decided to target two synagogues, the British consulate, and an HSBC Bank, all efforts to destroy Western interests.

Ozkan (2013), a Turkish police officer, presents, in a detailed study of the attacks performed by the AQT in Istanbul in November, 2003, the intelligence failure by Turkish agencies in preparing for and predicting them. By analyzing interviews with the terrorists, Ozkan explains how AQT was professional and well prepared for the attacks. The team used aliases, changing their passports continuously to avoid having official records of too many trips to Pakistan and Afghanistan. They wore modern clothing, including cutting their beards so that they would fit in with the public. They were extremely secretive to the point where some of the participants who were building the bombs did not know what the targets were or when they would be attacked (p. 162).

All four attacks occurred in Istanbul. On Saturday, November 15, the first truck exploded at the Neve Shalom Synagogue. Shortly after, the second truck exploded at the Beth Israel Synagogue. In total, 27 people were killed, including the two suicide bombers, Gokhan Elaltuntas and Mesut Cabuk, and 328 were hurt. On November 20, the third truck exploded in front of the HSBC bank. The fourth truck, shortly after, exploded in front of the British Consulate. On that day, 34 people were killed, including the two suicide bombers Ilyas Kuncak and Feridun Ugurlu, and about 450 people were injured (p. 137).

Ozkan describes the Istanbul bombings as an intelligence failure, which he defines as "the inability of intelligence community, as well as, policy makers to anticipate or prevent incidents that result in unexpected and undesired consequences" (p. 6). We can analyze this incident using the common methodology (risk assessment, methodology, and risk management) to better understand what the police did and didn't do before, during, and after the assaults took place.

Stage 1: Risk Assessment

As we explained at the outset, collecting and analyzing data are key steps in assessing risk. Data include information gathered through open sources, wiretapping, interrogations, informants, and reconnaissance (Ozkan, 2013, p. 12). Due to bureaucratic and legal roadblocks, Turkish law enforcement was unable to gather sufficient data to predict or prevent the November bombings. Turkey has three intelligence agencies: the Milli İstihbarat Teşkilatı (MIT), which is in charge of foreign and domestic intelligence gathering; the Gendarmerie, which is in charge of rural intelligence gathering; and the İstihbarat Dairesi Başkanlığı (IDB), which is in charge of domestic intelligence gathering (p. 180). According to Ozkan, the MIT and IDB compete for the best sources and share only limited information with each other (p. 187). Before the Istanbul bombings, both agencies were aware, through wiretapping and interrogations, of the existence of Muslim extremists living in Turkey and, had they cooperated with each other, they would have likely discovered the group before the attacks (p. 188).

Furthermore, the intelligence gathering process is limited by policies that restrict its effectiveness. First, suspects of terrorism can only be held for two days with a warrant, after which time they must be charged. Therefore, agencies only have 48 hours to obtain information through interrogations (p. 175). Communication interception is a last resort when collecting evidence and before 2005, it was very difficult to get approval to wiretap (p. 176). Therefore, Turkish agencies found it impossible to keep track of terrorist suspects over a long period of time (p.175). There was also no unit that gathered open source intelligence until 2008 (p. 198). Before the attacks, a journalist wrote an article in which he quoted one of the members of AQT who expressed his dissatisfaction with the Turkish government and his will to change it through any means necessary (p. 199). This information was not gathered by the police.

There is also no public support for intelligence. Ozkan describes how a private security guard was suspicious of *Gokkusagi* but did not report it to the police because he thought he would get in trouble (p. 186). In addition, before the attacks, there was no separate section of IDB that dealt specifically with Al Qaeda intelligence gathering. Instead, only two officers were in charge of gathering information about Al Qaeda and they reported to the section in charge of gathering information about radicalism, which directs attention to all groups with religious motives (p. 193).

The Turkish government did not finance intelligence well enough and actually decreased funding over time (p. 178). In addition, the counterterrorism policies were not well developed and, in Ozkan's opinion, there was not enough funding directed towards intelligence in regards to terrorist threats (p. 171).

There was no strategic intelligence occurring before the attacks. Ozkan claims that the Turkish agencies did not study patterns or attempt to assess the continued threat posed by Islamic extremists in and outside Turkey (p. 201). Further, they did not take into account that one of the synagogues that was bombed, Neve Shalom, had been attacked twice before and that it was a continued target for anti-Semitism

(p. 204). They were warned repeatedly by the US about Al Qaeda's interests in attacking countries that were allies with the West (p. 205). Despite the fact that 3,000 Turks had left the country to be trained in jihad, they did not believe themselves vulnerable to mass casualty attacks from these combatants (p. 203).

The lack of interagency cooperation extended internationally. While the US did warn Turkey about attacks in Istanbul, Ozkan argues that there was not enough information shared between the FBI, CIA, and Turkish agencies. For example, if CIA liaisons came to Turkey to gather intelligence about radicalism activities, they would not be given access to information from the MIT, which was in charge of international and domestic intelligence. They would instead be sent to the IDB that could not help them because it was in charge only of domestic intelligence and further did not want to share information with the CIA (p. 210). This lack of cooperation went both ways, and valuable information that could have led to the discovery of the AQT headquarters was not shared between agencies (p. 212).

Stage 2: Decision-Making

ICS was newly implemented in Turkey and was not fully prepared when responding to the attacks (Fratta, 2010, p. 366). Therefore, there was an unclear chain of command, and people did not understand their roles and responsibilities. Furthermore, communication between agencies, as well as the public, was not handled appropriately (p. 366). The media were the first at the scene of the bombings and reported live, showing graphic images. The government, in an attempt to control public panic, banned the news channels from the live broadcast. However, they did not replace this with their own reports, making people panic even more due to the lack of information being shared (p. 367). This resulted in people flocking to the scene and making phone calls that tied up the phone lines for six to eight hours after the attacks (p. 368).

After the first attack against the Neve Shalom and Beth Israel Synagogues, emergency responders were called to the scene to transport injured victims to hospitals around Istanbul. Firefighters and police were at the scenes of the attacks within minutes of the blasts. However, on both November 15 and 20, law enforcement personnel were only able to secure the area after 15 minutes, allowing uncontrolled movement by injured victims, media, and the public to and from the scene prior to their arrival. Medics also entered the bombed buildings before they were swept for secondary bombs and did so without protection. Furthermore, due to communication outages, large numbers of people drove to the site looking for loved ones, creating traffic jams which slowed ambulances from getting to the scene (p. 366). It was also reported that while ambulances were immediately dispatched on both days, on November 20, too many were sent, leaving the rest of Istanbul vulnerable if there had been a third attack (p. 367).

According to a study done by Rodoplu et al. (2005a), after the November 15 bombings, 76 out of 328 victims were brought to the American Hospital in Istanbul.

This specific hospital cared for the most victims of all the hospitals in Istanbul including hospitals that were much closer to the scene (p. 139). Only two injured victims arrived at the American Hospital within the hour of the attacks, 21 after an hour, 46 had no documented arrival time, and 7 were transferred from other hospitals after four hours (p. 138). Rodoplu et al. (2005a) criticize the emergency system in Istanbul stating that there is a "lack of central coordination of ambulance distribution according to changing hospital loads" and that there was a "lack of field triage, with ambulances simultaneously transporting seriously injured non-ambulatory victims and ambulatory victims with minor injuries" (p. 139).

Rodoplu et al. (2005a) also analyzed the impact of the bombings at the HSBC bank and the British consulate that occurred on November 20. After the attack, the Taksim Education and Research State Hospital (TERSH) received 184 victims in the first hour of the initial attack while the American Hospital received only 14. While the number of patients transported to care was more efficient than in the first attacks, "TERSH experienced an unprecedented demand for ED (emergency department) surge capacity in an open-air bombing" (Rodoplu et al., 2005b). They were prepared for this incident, though, as upon hearing of the attacks, TERSH immediately evacuated the first three floors of the hospital to make room for incoming victims (Fratta, 2010, p. 367). The authors state that in both cases, hospitalization and mortality rates were consistent with other open air mass casualty terrorist incidents (Rodoplu et al., 2005a, p. 139).

Stage 3: Risk Management

The Turkish police were able to identify and apprehend most of the people involved in the planning and implementation of the attacks within a month of the bombings (Ozkan, 2013, p. 140). In addition, they found 1,100 pounds of explosives that were to be used for future attacks in Istanbul (Fratta, 2010, p. 368).

Since the 2003 Istanbul bombings, the Turkish National Police created a Joint Intelligence Coordination Center where representatives of all three Turkish agencies meet to discuss intelligence (Ozkan, 2013, p. 188). Furthermore, a database was created to track all vehicles being sold, bought, and/or leased so that suspicious transactions can be flagged and investigated (p. 191). After 2003, international agencies are more cooperative with one another. The FBI has agreed to work with the Turkish National Police to help train them in intelligence including bringing Turkish police officers to the US to attend FBI training (p. 215).

Globally, Turkey, as well as other UN Member States, has, through the UN General Assembly, increased coordination efforts in counterterrorism (United Nations, 2013). In September 2006, Member States created a global strategy against terrorism called the United Nations Global Counter-Terrorism Strategy. As part of the plan of action, Member States agreed to increase cooperation and exchange information regarding terrorism and related crimes, such as drug trafficking, arms trafficking, money laundering, and smuggling of deadly materials including products to build nuclear weapons (UN General Assembly, 2006, p. 5). The resolution further considers the creation of an international center to fight terrorism and the creation of a single comprehensive database (p. 6).

In addition to signing the resolution, Turkey joined the Counter-Terrorism Committee (CTC) (Yavuz and Yildirim n.d.). The Ambassador and Permanent Representative of Turkey, Ertuğrul Apakan, served as chair for the Committee in 2010 (CTC, 2011). The CTC was established in response to the 9/11 attacks. It requested States to implement the following measures to combat terrorism:

- Criminalize the financing of terrorism
- Freeze without delay any funds related to persons involved in acts of terrorism
- Deny all forms of financial support for terrorist groups
- Suppress the provision of safe haven, sustenance, or support for terrorists
- Share information with other governments on any groups practicing or planning terrorist acts
- Cooperate with other governments in the investigation, detection, arrest, extradition, and prosecution of those involved in such acts
- Criminalize active and passive assistance for terrorism in domestic law and bring violators to justice (CTC, 2013)

In 2010, Turkey established the Anti-Terrorism Academy (ATAC) through the Turkish National Police to train local and international law enforcement about counterterrorist measures and strategies (TNP, 2013). Turkey continues to participate in and conduct counterterrorism training programs including training Afghan National Police in Turkey (UNDP, 2013).

In sum, this case study exemplifies translational approaches as it shows how information and data analysis can be used to overcome poorly coordinated prevention strategies and inadequate responses to threats. The efforts made to research the underlying factors that led to these attacks are important in guiding the ways in which agencies can improve their readiness and policies in managing the risks that come from terrorism.

Cybercrime

Background

Increased Internet penetration or the unhindered access to information can aid people with limited income in accessing information at low or no cost compared to print and broadcast information (Gercke, 2011). Unfortunately, the very same penetrating nature of the Internet that connects millions may compromise security, as it may create cyber-risks against society. For instance, in January 2010, Google announced the theft of its intellectual property (Markoff, Sanger, & Shanker, 2010), and in January 2012, Zappos, a US-based online shoe and apparel company, announced the theft of its customer information from its computer networks (Flegenheimer, 2012).

The financial loss attributed to cybercrime is enormous. According to Gercke (2011), in 2003, malicious software caused damages of up to $17 billion. In 2007, the $100 billion cybercrime revenue exceeded the illegal drug trade revenue for the first time. Further, 60 % of businesses in the US reported that cybercrime is more costly to them than physical crime (Gercke, 2011, p. 16).

Leaving the economic concerns aside, cyber-attacks against critical infrastructure, such as the 2003 Titan Rain attacks in the US, the 2007 cyber-attacks in Estonia, the 2008 cyber-attacks in Georgia, and the recent Stuxnet and Flame attacks in Iran, put cyber-attacks at the top of the security watch list on national and international agendas. In his statement published in the *New York Times* on July 26, 2012, General Keith B. Alexander, the Director of the National Security Agency and the Commander of the United States Cyber Command, acknowledged the increase in the number of attacks against US's critical infrastructure. He described the US's preparedness for a large attack on a scale of 1–10 (10 being the most prepared) as a 3 (Sanger & Schmitt, 2012).

The reality is that cyberspace is unregulated and chaotic. As no one owns it, no one truly regulates it. There have been efforts made by policy makers to address this chaos, but as the computer networks are global, it is only through international agreements that anything can really be done. In the meantime, it is simply up to corporations and government agencies to ensure that their own networks are secure. This is a daunting task but there are things that can be done while waiting for regulation to catch up to the developments in this area. Given the clandestine and borderless nature of cyber-threats, a collaborative response strategy informed by research is essential for an effective cybercrime strategy.

Stage 1: Risk Assessment and Cybercrime–Terror Continuum

Vulnerability to cybercrimes can be attributed to four risk factors: (1) the insider threat, (2) persistence of computer vulnerabilities, (3) errors in new software products, and (4) inadequate resources (Wilson, 2005). According to the "insider threat" argument, one of the biggest vulnerabilities of organizations to cyber-attack is the ease of copying and transferring data via a variety of portable storage devices, such as small flash drives. The second risk factor, "persistence of computer vulnerabilities," focuses on the targets of the crime:

> Vulnerabilities in software and computer system configurations provide entry points for a cyber-attack. Vulnerabilities persist largely as a result of poor security practices and procedures, inadequate training in computer security, or technical errors in software products (p. 14).

When considering the threats from "errors in new software products," software vendors are criticized for releasing software products that have errors that make the computer vulnerable to attacks (p. 14). Finally, despite this clear taxonomy of cyber-risks on paper, understanding cybercrime prevalence and using this information for risk assessment before and after critical cybercrime events is challenging and the resources to respond to these threats are limited.

The actual extent of cybercrime is unknown. There are many sources of data on cybercrime occurrences, such as national and international crime statistics and results of surveys conducted by the police, academic experts, international organizations, governments, and industries. However, there have been difficulties in integrating these data into cybercrime control strategies. These challenges are rooted in mainly three conditions: (1) methodological differences between data sources, (2) underreporting of offences, and (3) unreliable data collection methods.

Even if there are reliable cybercrime data sources on the local and global level, it is hard to incorporate these data due to differences in legislation and data collection practices. Underreporting may occur when businesses or governments do not provide information about security breaches as this might affect their reputation or highlight their weaknesses. Finally, Moitra (2005) states that cybercrimes are underrepresented in crime statistics due to the lack of systemization of recording for cybercrime types.

As Gercke concludes (2011), survey results of cybercrime are unreliable, as in many surveys, the accounts of financial losses and the number of recognized offenses are not justifiable. Furthermore, in many cases, unreliable and unverifiable information is repeatedly quoted. For instance, *TopTenReviews* estimates that Internet child pornography generates $2.5 billion annually worldwide without providing any information on their research methodology. In addition, with the increasing number of automated cyber-attacks, measuring cybercrime through traditional methods has become ineffective (Gercke, 2011, p. 39). When looking at the cybercrime–terror continuum, it is difficult to provide exact numbers of cyber-attacks that are cyber-terrorism in nature. Still, it is widely acknowledged that there is a link between cyber-criminals and terrorist groups that aids terror networks "to expand internationally through leveraging the computer resources, money laundering activities, or transit routes operated by criminals" (Wilson, 2008, p. 16).

According to Sieber and Brunst (2007), terrorist groups can use the Internet for various reasons. The Internet can be used to attack other IT infrastructure or physical objects, such as, landscape features, transportation vehicles, and people. It can act as a tool to disseminate terrorist content to partners, followers, and the public. For instance, according to the United States Institute of Peace, nearly all terrorist groups, including Hamas, Hezbollah, PKK, and Al Qaeda, maintain Web sites and use social media sites to communicate information (Gercke, 2011). Addressing the importance of the use of social media in terrorist acts, the Defense Advanced Research Projects Agency (DARPA) recently opened a solicitation to fund the development of a "software that can spot conflicts between groups and weak links that the Pentagon and law enforcement could exploit for 'strategic military operations' and espionage prevention" (GCN, 2012). The Internet is also a planning and surveillance instrument to access information such as satellite imagery and construction plans.

Stage 2: Decision-Making: Current Legislation and Legal Considerations in Regards to Combating Cybercrimes

According to a detailed chronology of the national cybercrime legislation by Goodman and Brenner (2002), the first wave of cybercrime legislation addresses data protection and citizens' rights to privacy. The second wave addresses the crimes that emerge due to the increasing reliance on computer systems and networks. The third and fourth waves aim to provide protection for intellectual property and against illegal and harmful content (pp. 33–34).

In 1983, the Organization for Economic Cooperation and Development (OECD) was the first to study the legal issues related to computer-related crime (Lovet, 2009). OECD made recommendations in an effort to harmonize the scope of cybercrimes in different national legal systems (Verdelho, 2008). In 1990, the United Nations addressed the legal problems posed by cybercrime and called Member States to:

> intensify their efforts to combat computer crime by modernizing their national criminal laws and procedures, improving computer security and prevention measures, and promoting the development of a comprehensive international framework of guidelines and standards for preventing, prosecuting, and punishing computer-related crime in the future (Goodman & Brenner, 2002, pp. 40–41).

In 1992, the Council of the OECD adopted the Recommendation of the Council Concerning Guidelines for the Security of Information Systems including laws, codes of conduct, technical measures, management and user practices, and public education provisions for security information systems (Goodman & Brenner, 2002, p. 41). In 1997, the G8 adopted a Ten-Point Action Plan including principles such as demolishing the safe havens for those who abuse information technologies; regardless of where harm has occurred, establishing coordination between all concerned states in the investigation and prosecution of international high tech crimes; and, training and updating law enforcement personnel who address high tech crimes (Gercke, 2011, p. 176).

The most global attempt to address cybercrime—with regard to the number of states involved in the process—has been the Convention on Cybercrime, drafted by the Council of Europe. The Convention aims to provide a legal framework for tackling cybercrime through the harmonization of cybercrime qualification and provision for laws, thus promoting better investigation capabilities and international cooperation (Lovet, 2009). Currently, the Council of Europe Convention on Cybercrime is still the only instrument supported by the majority of international organizations (Gercke, 2011). According to a Council of Europe statement, as of 2011, more than 100 countries signed, ratified, or used the Convention when drafting domestic legislation (Council of Europe, 2010).

Law enforcement, however, is not well equipped to deal with cybercrime as the transfer of human behavior into cyberspace has eroded four assumptions about real-world crime (Brenner, 2004, 2007a, 2007b). First, for a crime to occur we should have the target and the offender in a physically proximate space. Second, in real-world crime, the scale of the crime incident is small, in most cases as small as one-to-one: one offender and one target. Third, real-world crime is subject to some physical constraints. For instance, for a crime to occur the likely offender should have enough time and physical ability to commit the crime, and while doing that he should be involved in a minimum effort of planning and executing the crime. Fourth, targets, times, locations, and tactics of crime incidents follow a pattern. Based on these four assumptions, traditional law enforcement tactics suggest that crime investigations should focus on the physical scene of the crime in its geographical jurisdiction and utilize witnesses and crime scene evidence to identify the perpetrator and the harm inflicted on the victims (Brenner, 2004).

In the cyber world, however, crimes are not confined to any regional or national boundaries. Cyber-attacks can be committed by a person, a group of people, businesses, organizations, a government, or a computer in any part of the world against a person, group of people, businesses, organizations, a government, or a computer in any part of the world. Cybercrimes can harm these targets instantaneously, or over a longer period of time, without being noticed. Accordingly, the singular investigations of real-world crimes do not translate well into the investigation of cybercrimes.

A cybercrime initiated in several different countries increases the complexity of investigations and communication of data. The clandestine characteristic of cybercrime coupled with its borderless nature makes its investigation technically, culturally, and legally cumbersome. The crime scene, witnesses, and/or the evidence as we know it can disappear in a matter of minutes, long before cooperation to respond is established between the different authorities in different organizations, regions, or countries. Most of the time, a cybercrime investigation requires scrutiny of hardware, software, or data. This process may require authorization of higher levels of security clearance, which can be time consuming (Bednar, Katos, & Hennell, 2009). Furthermore, in every stage of a cybercrime prevention strategy, there are stakeholders from different organizations (government, businesses, nonprofit organizations) with uncommon priorities and missions. This can further complicate cooperation and the crime control efforts.

Cybercrimes can impose many other technical issues for the criminal justice system. On the technical level, cybercrimes can be troublesome first because of the difficulty of tracking cybercriminals who have used botnets[6] and fast flux networks.[7] Furthermore, it is impossible to prevent potential criminals from accessing information (Web sites explaining how to make a bomb, cybercriminal-cyber–terrorist communication Web sites, child pornography Web sites, etc.) as "tech-savvy" users will find ways around content filtering.

---

[6] A botnet is a group of computers that are used to generate viruses, spam, or flood a network with multiple requests to attempt to cause it failure (PCMAG, 2013a).

[7] A fast-flux network is a technique used to hide a cybercriminal's identity (IP address). This allows him/her to create a botnet that can join the network and then disappear before he/she can be traced (Whatis.com, 2013).

Stage 3: Risk Management

Depending on the target, governance in cyberspace may be maintained by active controllers (Internet users, corporate security organizations, state funded public/private policing organizations, law, and regulation), passive controllers (Internet service providers, decentralized command, and control of the Internet), or hybrid controllers (bureaucracies, government, and corporations as the collectors of records). While active controllers seek out the rule breakers, passive controllers arrange daily activities to assure conformity to active control (Newman & Clarke, 2003).

As active controllers, Internet users are encouraged to minimize their victimization risk by protecting personal information and by being in control of the usage of digital devices. In the fight against cyber-bullying, cyber-hate crimes, and identity theft, the National Cyber Security Alliance (NCSA) invites Internet users to share cyber responsibility. According to the NCSA Web site, in the case of identity theft, Internet users can minimize personal victimization risk by having the latest security software and automated software updates, protect all devices that can connect to the Internet, use security devices to scan external devices connected to the personal computers, and use security enabled Web sites while online shopping (NCSA, 2013).[8] To avoid cyber-violence such as cyber-bullying and harassment, NCSA invites parents to raise digital citizens by remaining positively engaged with children's online activity; supporting good online behavior; teaching critical thinking skills; explaining public nature of the Internet; reminding them to be good citizens by respecting personal information of friends, family, or any other person; keeping personal computers clean of malware; and, reviewing privacy settings of the Web sites children visit (NCSA, 2013).

As the keepers of client information, security departments of corporate organizations control the access to and transmission of personal information and electronic transmissions. State funded public/private policing organizations such as National Infrastructure Protection Center (NIPC) of the US or the National Criminal Intelligence Service (NCIS) of the UK protect critical infrastructure and monitor Internet activity (Newman & Clarke, 2003). Nevertheless, as exemplified by the national and international reaction to the recent NSA case, where the former NSA employee Edward Snowden revealed the details of NSA mass surveillance on foreigners and American citizens, government monitoring of Internet activity for security purposes can be a hot topic of criticism.

As explained in the section dedicated to decision-making, laws and regulations occupy an important place in minimizing the risk of cybercrime. Furthermore, passive controllers, such as Internet service providers, reduce cybercrime risk by setting standards and protocols for information exchange in cyberspace (Newman & Clarke, 2003).

---

[8] To see more about staying safe online, go to http://staysafeonline.org/stay-safe-online/protect-your-personal-information/id-theft-and-fraud.

In hybrid risk management, passive and active control mechanisms are applied at the same time. Management of the risk of child pornography appearing online provides a perfect example of such an approach. According to Wortley and Smallbone (2006), in the fight against Internet child pornography, a number of different risk control mechanisms are employed. For instance, to stop cyber child pornography, Internet Service Providers (ISPs) draft formal codes of conduct which bind members of a Web site not to accept illegal conduct on the ISPs' network. Such ISPs can provide hotlines to file complaints and apply filters to the browsers that their members use. Additionally, legislation holds ISPs responsible for site content, give authority to law enforcement to seize ISP accounts with a court order, and require user verification. Furthermore, some nonprofit organizations such as Wired Safety, Safeguarding Our Children—United Mothers (SOC-UM), and End Child Prostitution, Child Pornography and Trafficking of Children for Sexual Purposes (ECPAT) raise public awareness about cyber child pornography. Parents can also install filtering software on personal computers to regulate Internet content. Lastly, law enforcement mitigates the cyber child pornography risk including locating pornography sites, performing sting operations in chat rooms, and publicizing crackdowns.

Case Study: Risk Analysis of Stuxnet Cyber-Attack Using Common Methodology

In this section, we look at the risk factors related to one type of cybercrime, critical infrastructure infiltration via cyber-attacks against Supervisory Control and Data Acquisition (SCADA) systems. We specifically focus on the Stuxnet computer worm, which was used to attack Iran's nuclear facilities, to systemically analyze the risk components for attacks against SCADA systems. Although Stuxnet actually targeted the operators and not the SCADA controls themselves, we demonstrate the vulnerabilities associated with a SCADA system to show the effect it has (Langner, 2011, p. 49). Furthermore, we evaluate the risk management decisions for that particular attack. We discuss the issues that policy makers and law enforcement face when attempting to eliminate attacks against SCADA systems. Finally, we look at the conditions that led to the Stuxnet attack and evaluate the risk management decisions for this particular cyber-attack.

SCADA systems are computerized control systems that enable operators to remotely access real-time data and help carry out automated or manual commands to connected remote stations (Zhu, Joseph, & Sastry, 2011). As seen in Fig. 1.1, a typical SCADA system is made up of both hardware and software components. The system includes a master terminal unit (MTU), remote terminal units (RTU), communication equipment, and the system software. In a SCADA system, the communication equipment transfers the input and output between the MTU and the RTU whereas the software dictates the intervals and parameters for control and responses to abnormal parameters (Stouffer, Falco, & Scarfone, 2011).

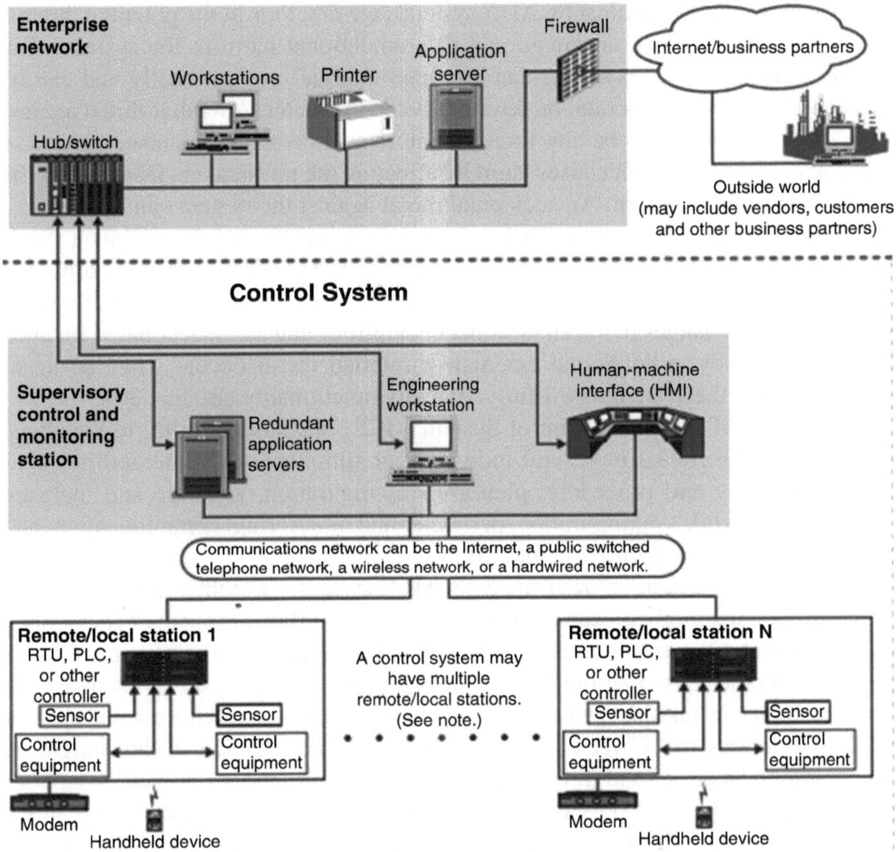

Fig. 1.1 Typical components of a control system. *Source*: USGAO (2004)

SCADA systems are chosen as a case study for a very particular reason. Compared to a variety of other cyber-attacks, the attacks against SCADA systems at critical infrastructures pose significantly more devastating consequences as these systems are commonly used to regulate water, wastewater, oil, gas, electrical power, and transportation operations. Therefore, attacks against a particular SCADA system that controls a critical infrastructure might “endanger public health and safety, damage the environment, or cause a loss of production, generation, or distribution by public utilities” for millions (USGAO, 2004, p. 2). Unlike IT systems where protecting the central host is more important than the edge client, in SCADA systems, protecting the field devices is as of equal importance to protecting the central host. The SCADA systems, with their extensive use in critical infrastructures as hard real-time systems, exert a greater threat in more remote geographies with a direct impact on persons and their surroundings.

To analyze the risk against SCADA systems, we first look at the potential threats. Who or what can cause an intentional or unintentional harm to the system? The threats against SCADA systems can originate internally or externally and can be accidental, natural, deliberate, or deteriorative in character. A natural threat against a SCADA system might be any force of nature such as an earthquake, a storm, a hurricane, and a flood that causes harm by affecting the physical environment or the components of the system. An accidental threat against the system can be an external or internal agent that causes harm to system components with no intent. Such harm can be due to negligence or human error. A deteriorative threat harms the system not at once but gradually over time due to lack of maintenance of system components or changes in the environment conditions that are unaccounted for such as erosion. Lastly, a deliberate external or internal threat occurs when an agent causes harm to the system to willfully affect its functionality (Boone, 2013).

In the case of Industrial Control Systems (ICS), the susceptibility to the above threats might be rooted in several individual or simultaneous vulnerabilities connected to policy and procedure, platform's configuration, software and malware protection, network's configuration, perimeter and monitoring, communication, and wireless connection (Stouffer et al., 2011).

According to Boone (2013), in a SCADA system—which is an example of ICS—these vulnerabilities can be organized into five related groups: (1) personnel, (2) procedural, (3) operational, (4) technical, and (5) physical. These vulnerabilities are nested in the sense that the level of susceptibility in one group can increase the level of threat in another group. Personnel vulnerability can cause accidental or deliberate threats to SCADA systems. For instance, a SCADA system might be vulnerable to an accidental threat because of the lack of training or lack of supervision of personnel. A SCADA system might also be vulnerable to a deliberate threat because of the lack of proper security clearance of personnel. As stated by Boone (2013), among all other threats, institutional personnel threats require more scrutiny since "many of the other vulnerabilities could cascade and be exasperated due to weaknesses at the level of the individual" (p. 67).

Procedural vulnerabilities include any shortcomings in process. These may involve a lack of up-to-date, consistent, harmonious, and unified policies, standards, and directives that can assist personnel addressing day-to-day operations and emergency conditions. Operational vulnerabilities arise when personnel are not qualified enough to perform operations due to lack of directions or training. Such operational vulnerabilities include lack of alignment in individual processes, lack of training in hazard prevention, lack of cross-training to fulfill duties of key personnel in their absence, lack of institutional communication, and lack of preserving of confidentiality of operations (p. 68).

Technical vulnerabilities include easy penetrating IT systems, the integration of SCADA networks with other networks, inadequate configuration management, inappropriate clipping levels to set off an alarm in the case of an anomaly, and infrequent maintenance of the equipment associated with the SCADA systems. Lastly, physical vulnerabilities include anything that makes the SCADA systems penetrable due to the lack of physical security of the system, such as an inadequate access control, lack of physical barriers in the system perimeter, and not locking or controlling the valued assets and the rooms in which they are held (p. 69).

The Stuxnet Case Study

Stuxnet is a computer worm that was originally deployed to physically destroy a military target, the Natanz uranium enrichment facility in Iran, in hopes of disabling Iran's nuclear program (Langner, 2011). Launched in the 1950s, Iran's nuclear program was delayed until the early 1990s because of the 1979 revolution and the Iran–Iraq war. The continuation of the program became public when the National Council of Resistance of Iran (NCRI), the exiled opposition group, announced the presence of a uranium enrichment facility at Natanz and a heavy water production facility at Arak (Reuters, 2005). Although Iran insisted on the peaceful nature of its nuclear program, after inspections, the International Atomic Energy Agency (IAEA) reported on Iran's noncompliance with the Nuclear Non-Proliferation Treaty (NPT) at these facilities. Iran opened its facilities for inspection by the United Nations and promised to suspend their operation in 2004. Nevertheless, since former President Mohammed Khatami's highly criticized decision to resume some activity at these facilities in 2005, Iran has been suspected of developing nuclear weapons.

The role of SCADA systems in the Stuxnet attack has elicited different theories. For instance, according to Marks (2011), Stuxnet "exploited vulnerabilities in Microsoft Windows to give a remote hacker the ability to inject malicious code into a market-leading PLC (Programmable Logic Controller) made by German electronics conglomerate Siemens." On the other hand, according to Langner (2011):

> ... a SCADA application played a small role in the Stuxnet attack, but mainly as a means of distribution. The real attack wasn't against SCADA software—it was aimed at industrial controllers that might or might not be attached to a SCADA system (p. 49).

The Stuxnet worm was detected in early July 2010, but different variants of the worm were confirmed to have existed in 2009, and probably even earlier (Falliere, Murchu, & Chien, 2011). Stuxnet was programmed to find and exploit Microsoft Windows' vulnerabilities by allowing a hacker access to Siemens' PLC. The assailant programmed malicious code that *selectively* attacked the Iranian uranium enrichment facility (Marks, 2011). According to the Symantec estimates, however, the worm also indiscriminately spread to Indonesia, India, Azerbaijan, the USA, Pakistan, and other countries (Shearer, 2013). According to a detailed Symantec report on Stuxnet, the worm contained many features, such as:

> replicating itself through removable drives, spreading in a local area network (LAN), spreading through server message block (SMB), copying and executing itself on remote computers and Step 7 projects, updating itself through a peer-to-peer mechanism within a LAN, contacting a command and control server, attempting to bypass security products, fingerprinting a specific ICS and modifying code on the Siemens PLCs, and hiding modified code on PLCs (Falliere et al., 2011, p. 2).

Stuxnet is believed to have destroyed 1,000 (11 %) of the centrifuges at Natanz when it was deployed. These failures had a significant overall effect on Iran's nuclear program and decreased production of enriched uranium (Mueller & Yadegari, 2012, p. 1). In the next subsections, following the common methodology framework, we will examine the risk assessment, decision-making, and risk management stages for the analysis of the Stuxnet attack.

Stage 1: Risk Assessment

The Natanz plant's increased vulnerability to the Stuxnet attack was explained by several risk factors that can fit into the scope of the "insider threat." A worm like Stuxnet must be placed on an external drive and inserted into a PC before it can be activated. Therefore, the lack of a control mechanism for use of removable drives in SCADA systems by the Natanz employees was a fundamental vulnerability in SCADA systems. As explained earlier, according to the "insider threat" argument, one of the biggest vulnerabilities of organizations to cyber-attack is the ease of copying and transferring data via a variety of portable storage devices. In the Stuxnet attack, the malicious software was delivered to the Iranian nuclear plant Natanz on a thumb drive (Terdiman, 2012). Stuxnet's success in infiltrating the system was attributed to its superior ability in bypassing the antivirus software by making the program resemble legitimate software (Falliere et al., 2011; Mueller & Yadegari, 2012).

Stuxnet was undetected for more than a year or two due to the simultaneous exploitation of three vulnerabilities: (1) the use of hardcoded default passwords in SCADA systems for internal inter-process communication, (2) the ease of use of the classical Windows rootkit in Stuxnet, and (3) zero-day flaws within all Windows operation systems (K2E Security, 2013). Stuxnet remained undetected because it used legitimate digital signatures of Realtek Semiconductor Corp and JMicron Technology Corp. With these stolen certificates, Stuxnet successfully blended in with the authenticated programs. Stuxnet exploited Siemens's "default password" policy, which advised Siemens WinCC SCADA system users to log onto the SCADA database using the default password that was publicly available on two blog sites at the time of the attack (K2E Security, 2013). Finally, Stuxnet successfully used four Windows zero-day exploits. Zero-day exploits, also known as zero-day flaws, refer to the exploit of the security vulnerability of a system on the same day that that vulnerability is discovered. In other words, these types of vulnerabilities have no patch software to fix problems, as they are newly discovered vulnerabilities.[9] Accordingly, such vulnerability can continue harming a system from the day it is discovered to the day a patch is released.

---

[9] Patch software is "A fix to a program. In the past, a patch used to mean changing actual executable, machine instructions, but today more often than not, it means replacing an executable module in its entirety such as an .EXE or .DLL file. A profusion of patches to an application implies that its logic was poorly designed in the first place." (PCMAG, 2013b)

Stage 2: Decision-Making

As indicated earlier, the US and Israel were accused of being the originators of the Stuxnet attacks. According to Michael Joseph Gross, a contributing editor to *Vanity Fair*, Stuxnet, "is the new face of 21st-century warfare: invisible, anonymous, and devastating" (Gross, 2011). Cyber-attacks similar to Stuxnet are traced back to nation states, really the only entity large enough to mount these types of attacks. In addition, these types of "drone-like" worm attacks can paralyze the functions of modern life for hundreds of millions of people through SCADA systems.

A cyber-terrorism attack differs from other forms of cyber-attacks in its political intent. In many instances, the term "cyber-terrorism" is used interchangeably with the term "cyber-warfare," as cyber-warfare is essentially the utilization of ICTs in conducting warfare against a political body using the Internet. However, although exploitation of ICTs in cyber-attacks, cyber-terrorist attacks, or cyber-warfare may resemble one another, they are legally different (Gercke, 2011, p. 116).

In the case of Stuxnet, the decision-making process was limited. This type of worm was unique, thus no clear guidelines on how to address such an attack existed. The response process further slowed down due to a lack of intercompany cooperation. According to an interview with Sergey Ulasen, the person who discovered Stuxnet in June 2010, the Stuxnet worm surfaced when a customer in Iran reported arbitrary stop errors and computer reboots. Upon an initial analysis of the problem, Ulasen's then-employer VirusBlokAda, a Belarusian antivirus company, first decided to inform only the parties involved. With neither the resources nor the connections in the industry for the analysis of such a malware, the company failed to bring the two key decision-makers, Microsoft and Realtek, to the table. Ulasen then decided to publish reports about the malware on the Web sites of VirusBlokAda and a popular industry forum. Once industry experts started to pay attention, the speculations related to the connection between the malware, SCADA systems, and Iran's nuclear program arose. In the meantime, with the help of Andreas Marx, the CEO of AV-TEST GmbH, Ulasen succeeded in getting the Microsoft Security Center to conduct a thorough analysis of the case (Kaspersky, 2011).

Right after the global recognition of this particular attack, Iran denied the connection of Stuxnet as the cause of the delay in launching its first nuclear plant. Iran's response could be due to a number of reasons. Among these, Iran suspected Stuxnet to be an Israeli weapon and may not have wanted to ackowledge that it was successful (Brown, 2011, pp. 71–73).

Stage 3: Risk Management

Following the discovery of the Stuxnet worm, Siemens and Microsoft began offering patches to resolve the problems with the PLCs and zero-day flaws. Users were also advised against third-party USB devices. To address the stolen certificate issue, VeriSign revoked the Realtek and JMicron certificates. In response to the Stuxnet attack, many companies including Symantec published best practices guidelines on topics including the proper use of a firewall and password policies, level of user privilege, automatic launch of executable files, file sharing, patch updates, employee training, and steps to follow in case of an emergency. In addition, in 2011, Iran announced the establishment of a cyber police unit (Karimi, 2011).

In terms of research and development, companies like Innominate Security Technologies AG in Berlin are working on solutions to beef up security and decrease vulnerabilities of SCADA systems and computers in general (Rössel, 2011). Innominate developed a device called the mGuard which was available in 2009, before Stuxnet was launched. In fact, according to a study conducted at the University of East Westphalia-Lippe in Germany, had the mGuard CIFS Integrity Monitoring device been put in place on the Iranian computers infected by Stuxnet, they would have recognized the Stuxnet infections on the day it was installed. It would have revealed the "unexpected manipulations by the worm and warned asset operators about them long before any commercial antivirus product" (p. 34). The functionalities of the mGuard include encrypted VPN tunneling, router, firewall, integrity, and authentication monitoring (p. 33).

In summary, the global challenges of cybercrime have provoked some real dangers for individuals and businesses who find it difficult to keep up with the innovations of cybercrooks and find that there are few resources to help protect them from attacks. How this will play out as we become more virtual in all of our transactions (social, economic, and political) promises an interesting future for policy makers and enforcement agencies tasked with responding to these threats.

Part IV. Global Risks and Local Response: Program Development and Policy Implications

The success of response in a policy environment committed to translational approaches depends on a commitment to evaluation that documents what works and what does not. With the large expenditures in law enforcement and counterterrorism, it is important to determine the overall success of interventions. In this way, good programs can be augmented and programs that don't work can be eliminated. In reflecting on their original research on the lack of evaluation of counterterrorism programs, Lum and Kennedy (2012) point out that the excuses for failing to determine the effectiveness of intervention come from myths that are used to justify the inability to account for rare events, such as terrorism, the need for secrecy, the inability to experiment, and the urgency to respond. These limitations exist, and we have documented many of them in this brief. But, what we learned from police research, where these same limitations were often touted over the years as reasons for not applying systematic review to enforcement decisions, is that the advent of improved data access and innovative analytics has dramatically improved police practice and effectiveness. No longer are police operating in a vacuum, relying only on their instincts and past efforts. They are subject to continuous monitoring and assessment that is used to support and justify their decisions.

The need for transparency in effort and impact derives from the need to be better prepared to manage local impacts. The successes of applied police research need to be extended beyond crime outcomes and encompass the global factors that impact on strategies for response. Therefore, we add to the need for evaluation of counterterrorism strategies, espoused by Lum and Kennedy, the idea that these responses are linked to crime prevention and that global threats can only be mitigated through local responses that work.

In this brief, we analyzed the nature of cybercrime and terrorism. Each of these crimes affects both international and local laws, law enforcement, and communities. These crimes also share common trends, including crossing of tangible borders (in terms of country and states lines) and proverbial borders (in terms of computers and Internet). Furthermore, each crime can attack the security of a nation and is, therefore, dealt with by creating laws to keep people (or viruses) out.

However, while these acts of crime and terrorism threaten the freedom and security of nations and communities, policy makers and law enforcement must be aware of the complexities that arise when dealing with such crimes. When policy is written, human rights and civil liberties for the thousands of innocents must not be ignored to capture the few criminals. It is also prudent for nations to look at international law and laws passed by other countries, such as the ECHR law for torture, as models for creating effective and fair policy prescriptions.

In terms of extended research, international and local organizations must work together to deal with such issues. As stated before, cybercrime and terrorism are problems that can cross borders, thus breaching both national and local security. Perpetrators and victims of these crimes may regularly be in contact with citizens of the destination country and are putting nationals, and foreign nationals, at risk. Tracking and monitoring these activities must, therefore, be done on international, national, and local levels to prevent and mitigate these issues. Through partnership and communal standards for recording and keeping data on such crimes, information can be collected that may allow researchers to better understand the scope of these issues. Furthermore, data will shed light onto the effectiveness of laws and policy.

Lum and Kennedy (2012) outline key steps that could be followed in increasing our understanding of how interventions can be evaluated in terms of their effectiveness in addressing threats. This involves developing a research infrastructure that includes the following activities, modeled after suggestions for improvements to counterterrorism approaches in the US:

- Changing agency focus and research portfolios related to terrorism away from technology development and more towards methodologically rigorous outcome evaluations of existing interventions.
- Continuing to explore alternative methods of evaluation, especially for rare events but, in addition, we would add a need to develop better monitoring tools for high frequency, but clandestine, crime, such as the drug trade and human trafficking.
- Developing discourse and research around evaluation goals, including standards for data reporting, definitional analysis, systematic reviews of research, and finding ways to link etiology research to evaluation research.
- Creating access routes for researchers to both classified and unclassified data.
- Improving and increasing dialogue between researchers, policy makers, and practitioners, including overcoming myths, fears, and uncertainties about the intentions and capabilities of all three groups.
- Building into public policies and laws requirements for evaluation of those policies.
- Developing mechanisms of both delivery and interpretation of research evaluation results to practitioners and policy makers.
- Basing agent and bureaucratic performance on measureable outcomes and third-party assessments.
- Enhancing academic training and support for new scholars who are interested in studying within these areas but are fearful of risks to publication and tenure.
- Developing research dissemination and reviewing frameworks to make sense of growing amounts of research in this area (pp. 374–375).

As Lum and Kennedy argue, the development of evaluation research in policing since the 1970s has led to important discoveries about the effectiveness and ineffectiveness of commonly used interventions. It is on the basis of the development of evidence-based translational approaches that connect research to practice that progress can be made in understanding global threats and their impact on local society.

As we discussed extensively in this book, most risks, although pertaining to a specific locality or nation, directly or indirectly affect other regions and countries, as well. We emphasize that risk can be looked at as systemic and its management can be facilitated through cooperation between governments who agree on a common methodology for assessment and governance. However, there is still work to be done in developing ways in which threats can be monitored and their consequences reduced. As Kennedy et al. (2011) suggest, the requirements for adopting a common methodology include:

- The ample and efficient risk management at a local level
- The efficient and unstrained communication of risk data across different levels of the same organization and different organizations
- A "common consent" risk identification and prioritization
- (The existence of) parties eager to take responsibility for risk
- Long-term dedications for risk management
- An "all satisfying" risk response (Kennedy et al., 2011, p. 50)

Among these factors, *the limited access to information, resources, power, and structures* constitute the root causes of vulnerability to any risks. Accordingly the resistance to risk necessitates a programmatic approach involving ongoing and iterative risk assessment strategy. This may be implemented by involving different stakeholders, such as international standardizing bodies (e.g., WHO, 2009), national governments, private and public institutions, and local communities.

> Although, in general, the localities affected by the risks are perceived as the main responsible parties of risk management, when the systemic nature of risks are taken into consideration the general frame of directions and resources should be allocated by the organizations in the higher levels of risk management (such as governments, national organizations or international organizations). It is at this level of initial directions that standardizes the assessment; planning and development strategies will ease the communication of information between different levels of the risk management hierarchy (Kennedy et al., 2011, p. 50).

Future Challenges in Applying Common Methodology to Global Threats

The two examples that we presented above demonstrate the ways in which translational approaches can be programmed to anticipate and manage global threats at local levels. What is noteworthy in these approaches is that the common methodology perspective appears effective in laying out a framework for assessment and response in these low frequency but high impact events, LFHI (terrorism or cyber attacks), despite the difficulties involved in anticipating them due to their infrequent occurrence. The ability to identify a specific threat and use it as an example of best practice in the future makes the integration of analysis into decision-making and prevention strategies more straightforward.

A different set of challenges appear when dealing with high frequency, low impact events (HFLI). These are threats that, by themselves have limited impact, but because they happen often, they pose serious difficulties for local law enforcement. When we consider the local effects of transnational organized crime, drugs importation, illegal migration, and human trafficking, each of these problems originates from a complex set of conditions that defy easy classification. In addition, responses are poorly coordinated, information is hard to come by, and the impacts are hard to judge. There is, as well, as is the case with LFHC events, a disconnect between the global and local initiatives developed to control these types of problems but the diffuse nature of these incidents creates serious difficulties in managing results.

The obvious need to expand our thinking about managing global threats from drugs or trafficking in ways that are similar to terrorism or cybercrime is compromised by the disconnect between the global reality of the drug and human trafficking trade. The realities of local law enforcement who must deal with the consequences of these global forces creates an imperative for researchers and policy makers to more directly connect the global to the local. This is the future challenge for translational approaches.

References

Appell, D. (2001). Precautionary principle: The new uncertainty principle. *Scientific American* 18–19.
Aronofsky, D., & Cooper, M. (2009). The war on terror and international human rights: Does Europe get it right. *Denver Journal of International Law and Policy, 37*(4), 567–613.
Anarumo, M. (2011). Threats, vulnerability, and exposure to terrorism: The practitioner's view of terrorism threat. In L. W. Kennedy & E. F. McGarrell (Eds.), *Crime and terrorism risk* (pp. 54–79). New York: Routledge.
Beck, U. (1992). *Risk society: Towards a new modernity*. Thousand Oaks, CA: Sage.
Bednar, P. M., Katos, V., & Hennell, C. (2009). On the complexity of collaborative cyber crime investigations. *Digital Evidence and Electronic Signature Law Review, 6*, 214–219.
Björnehed, E. (2004). Narco-terrorism: The merger of the war on drugs and the war on terror. *Global Crime, 6*(3&4), 305–324.
Bouchard, M., & Wilkins, C. (2009). *Illegal markets and the economics of organized crime*. New York: Routledge.
Boone, W. (2013). Risk management. In R. Radvanovsky & J. Brodsky (Eds.), *Handbook of SCADA/control systems security* (pp. 41–83). Boca Raton, FL: CRC Press.
Brané, M., & Lundholm, C. (2008). Human rights behind bars: Advancing the rights of immigration detainees in the United States through human rights frameworks. *Immigration Law Journal, 22*(2), 147–175.
Brenner, S. W. (2004). Toward a criminal law for cyberspace: A new model of law enforcement? *Rutgers Computer and Technology Law Journal, 30*, 1–104.
Brenner, S. W. (2007a). Private-public sector cooperation in combating cybercrime: In search of a model. *Journal of International Commercial Law and Technology,* 2(2), 58–67.
Brenner, S. W. (2007b). At light speed: Attribution and response to cybercrime/terrorism/warfare. *Journal of Criminal Law and Criminology, 97*(2), 379–476.
Brown, G. D. (2011). Why Iran didn't admit Stuxnet was an attack. *Joint Force Quarterly, 63*, 70–73. Retrieved from http://www.ndu.edu/press/lib/images/jfq-63/JFQ63_70-73_Brown.pdf.
Campbell Collaborative. (2013). Retrieved from http://www.campbellcollaboration.org/crime_and_justice/index.php
Caplan, J., & Kennedy, L. W. (2011). *Risk terrain modelling manual*. Newark, NJ: Rutgers Center on Public Security.
Carter, D. L., & Carter, J. G. (2009). The intelligence fusion process for state, local, and tribal law enforcement. *Criminal Justice and Behavior, 36*, 1323–1339.
Carter, J., & Chermak, S. (2012). Evidence-based intelligence practices: Examining the role of fusion centers as a critical source of information. In C. Lum & L. W. Kennedy (Eds.), *Evidence-based counterterrorism policy* (pp. 65–88). New York: Springer.

L.W. Kennedy et al., *Translational Criminology and Counterterrorism: Global Threats and Local Responses*, SpringerBriefs in Criminology, DOI 10.1007/978-1-4614-5556-1, © The Author 2014

CE (Council of Europe). (2010). *Information documents SG/Inf(2010)4*. Salvador, Brazil. Retrieved April 14, 2013 from http://www.coe.int/t/dghl/standardsetting/t-cy/T-CY%20Bureau%20(2010)%20SG%20Inf(2010)4.pdf

Cha, V. D. (2000). Globalization and the study of international security. *Journal of Peace Research, 37*(3), 391–403.

CIA. (2013). *The world factbook 2013–14*. Washington, DC: Central Intelligence Agency. Retrieved from https://www.cia.gov/library/publications/the-world-factbook/index.html.

Cohen, D. H. (2010). Post-9/11 anti-terrorism policy regarding noncitizens and the constitutional idea of equal protection under the laws. *Texas Law Review, 88*(6), 1323–1343.

Cole, D. (2003). *Enemy aliens: Double standards and constitutional freedoms in the war on terrorism*. New York: The New Press.

CTC (Counter-Terrorism Committee). (2011). *CTC Chairman biographical note, Ertuğrul Apakan*. Security Council. Retrieved from https://www.un.org/en/sc/ctc/bio_apakan.html

CTC (Counter-Terrorism Committee). (2013). *Our mandate*. Security Council. Retrieved from https://www.un.org/en/sc/ctc/index.html

Curtis, G. E., & Karacan, T. (2002). *The nexus among terrorists, narcotics traffickers, weapons proliferations, and organized crime networks in Western Europe*. Washington, DC: Library of Congress.

Dandurand, Y. & V. Chin. (2004). *Links between terrorism and other forms of crime*. Retrieved from http://www.icclr.law.ubc.ca/publications/reports/tnoc_links_study_report.pdf

Davis, L. E. (2003). Globalization's security implications. *RAND Issue Paper*. Retrieved from http://www.rand.org/pubs/issue_papers/IP245.html

Davison, A. (2003). Turkey, a 'secular' state? The challenge of description. *South Atlantic Quarterly, 102*(2/3), 333–350.

Dishman, C. (2001). Terrorism, crime, and transformation. *Studies in Conflict and Terrorism, 24*(1), 43–58.

Doğruel, F., & Leman, J. (2009). 'Conduct' and 'counterconduct' on the southern border of Turkey: Multicultural Antakya. *Middle Eastern Studies, 45*(4), 596–610.

Falliere, N., Murchu, L. O., & Chien, E. (2011). *W32.Stuxnet Dossier*. Retrieved from http://www.wired.com/images_blogs/threatlevel/2011/02/Symantec-Stuxnet-Update-Feb-2011.pdf

FBI (Federal Bureau of Investigation). (2008). *Fact sheet: Justice Department counter-terrorism efforts since 9/11*. Washington, DC: Department of Justice.

FEMA (Federal Emergency Management Agency). (2013). Incident command system. Retrieved from http://www.fema.gov/incident-command-system

Ferguson, Y. H., & Mansbach, R.W. (2012). *Globalization: The return of borders to a borderless world*. NY: Routledge.

Flegenheimer, M. (2012). Zappos says hackers may have accessed customer account details. *NY Times*, January 16. Retrieved from http://bits.blogs.nytimes.com/author/matt-flegenheimer/

Fratta, A. (2010). Post-9/11 responses to mass casualty bombings in Europe: Lessons, trends and implications for the United States. *Studies in Conflict and Terrorism, 33*(4), 364–385.

Gawande, A. (2013, April 17). Why Boston's hospitals were ready. *The New Yorker*. Retrieved fromhttp://www.newyorker.com/online/blogs/newsdesk/2013/04/why-bostons-hospitals-were-ready.html

GCN. (2012, July 31). DOD wants cyberterrorism-prediction software. Retrieved from http://gcn.com/articles/2012/07/31/agg-dod-small-biz-software-support.aspx

Gercke, M. (2011). *Understanding cybercrime: A guide for developing countries*. International Telecommunication Union. Retrieved from http://www.itu.int/ITU-D/cyb/cybersecurity/docs/ITU_Guide_A5_12072011.pdf

Gerring, J. (2001). *Social science methodology: A critical framework*. Cambridge, England: Cambridge University Press.

Gerring, J. (2010). *Social science methodology: Tasks, strategies, criteria*. Cambridge, England: Cambridge University Press.

Goodman, M. D., & Brenner, S. W. (2002). Emerging consensus on criminal conduct in cyberspace. *International Journal of Law and Information Technology, 10*(2), 139–223.

Gottschalk, P. (2009). Value configurations in organised crime. *Policing & Security, 19*(1), 47–57.
Gross, J. M. (2011, April). *A declaration of cyber-war. Vanity Fair*. Retrieved from http://www.vanityfair.com/culture/features/2011/04/stuxnet-201104
Haller, M. H. (1990). Illegal enterprise: A theoretical and historical interpretation. *Criminology, 28*(2), 207–235.
Herman, M., McDonald, J., & Mastny, V. (2006). Did intelligence matter in the Cold War? *Forsvarsstudier.*
Hutchinson, S., & O'Malley, P. (2007). A crime–terror nexus? Thinking on some of the links between terrorism and criminality. *Studies in Conflict Terrorism, 30*(12), 1095–1107.
Ikenberry, G. J. (2003). Review of the book *Distant proximities: Dynamics beyond globalization* by J.M. Rosenau. *Foreign Affairs*. Retrieved from http://www.foreignaffairs.com/articles/59217/g-john-ikenberry/distant-proximities-dynamics-beyond-globalization
Jenkins, W. (2007). Homeland security: Preparing for and responding to disasters. In *Testimony before the Subcommitte on Homeland Security, Committee on Appropriations, House of Representatives*. Washington, DC: GAO.
K2E Security. (2013). Analysis of the Siemens SCADA and Windows shortcut vulnerabilities. Retrieved from http://www.k2esec.com/vulnerabilities/what-is-really-the-concern-with-the-scada-vulnerability
Karimi, N. (2011, March 14). Report: Iran's paramilitary launches cyber attack. *Washington Post*. Retrieved from http://www.washingtonpost.com/wpdyn/content/article/2011/03/14/AR2011031401029.html
Kaspersky, E. (2011, November 2). The man who found stuxnet- sergey ulasen in the spotlight. *Nota Bene*. Retrieved from http://eugene.kaspersky.com/2011/11/02/the-man-who-found-stuxnet-sergey-ulasen-in-the-spotlight/
Kennedy, L. W., Marteache, N., & Gaziarifoglu, Y. (2011). Understanding scalability of risk, global risk assessment: The search for a common methodology. In L. W. Kennedy & E. F. McGarrell (Eds.), *Crime and terrorism risk studies in criminology and criminal justice* (pp. 29–53). New York: Routledge.
Kotz, D. (2013, April 24). *Injury toll from Marathon bombs reduced to 264*. The Boston Globe. Retrieved April 29, 2013.
LaFree, G. (2012). Generating terrorism event databases: Results from the global terrorism database, 1970 to 2008. In C. Lum & L. W. Kennedy (Eds.), *Event-based counterterrorism policy* (pp. 41–64). New York: Springer.
LaFree, G., Yang, S. M., & Crenshaw, M. (2009). Trajectories of terrorism. *Criminology and Public Policy, 8*(3), 445–473.
Langner, R. (2011). Stuxnet: Dissecting a cyberwarfare weapon. *IEEE Security and Privacy, 9*(3), 49–51.
Laub, J. H. (2011). What is translational criminology. *NIJ Journal, 268*, 16–21.
Lieberman, E. S. (2010). Bridging the qualitative-quantitative divide: Best practices in the development of historically oriented replication databases. *Annual Review of Political Science, 13*, 37–59.
Loder, A. & Deprez, E. E. (2013, April 19). Boston bombing victim in photo helped identify suspects. *Bloomberg*. Retrieved from http://www.bloomberg.com/news/2013-04-19/boston-bombing-victim-in-iconic-photo-helped-identify-attackers.html
Lovet, G. (2009). *Fighting cybercrime: Technical, juridical and ethical challenges*. Retrieved July 06, 2013 from http://www.fortiguard.com/files/VB2009_Fighting_Cybercrime_-_Technical, Juridical_and_Ethical_Challenges.pdf
Lum, C., & Kennedy, L. W. (2012). Evidence-based counterterrorism policy. In L. W. Kennedy & C. Lum (Eds.), *Evidence-based counterterrorism policy* (pp. 1–3). New York: Springer.
Lum, C., Kennedy, L. W., & Sherley, A. (2006). Are counter-terrorism strategies effective? The results of the Campbell systematic review on counter-terrorism evaluation research. *Journal of Experimental Criminology, 2*(4), 489–516.
Lustick, I. (2006). *Trapped in the war on terror*. Philadelphia: University of Pennsylvania Press.

Markoff, J., Sanger, D. E., & Shanker, T. (2010, January 25). In digital combat, U.S. finds no easy deterrent. *New York Times*. Retrieved from http://www.nytimes.com/2010/01/26/world/26cyber.html?_r=1&pagewanted=all

Marks, P. (2011, January). Why the Stuxnet worm is like nothing seen before. *New Scientist*. Retrieved from http://www.newscientist.com/article/dn19504-why-the-stuxnet-worm-is-like-nothing-seen-before.html?full=true#.UdOiavm1HTA

Matarese, J. (2013, April 18). Security meeting held for Long Island Marathon after bombings. *ABC*. Retrieved from http://abclocal.go.com/ktrk/story?section=news/local/long_island&id=9066594

Merola, L. M. (2012). Evaluating the legal challenges and effects of counterterrorism policy. In C. Lum & L. W. Kennedy (Eds.), *Evidence-based counterterrorism policy* (pp. 281–300). New York: Springer.

Moitra, S. D. (2005). Developing policies for cybercrime: Some empirical issues. *European Journal of Crime, Criminal Law and Criminal Justice, 13*(3), 435–464.

Mueller, J. (2006). *Overblown*. New York: Free Press.

Mueller, P. & Yadegari, B. (2012). The Stuxnet Worm. Retrieved March 15, 2013 from http://www.cs.arizona.edu/~collberg/Teaching/466566/2012/Resources/presentations/2012/topic9-final/report.pdf.

National Commission on Terrorist Attacks Upon the United States. (2004). *The 9/11 commission report: Final report of the National Commission on Terrorist Attacks upon the United States*. Washington, DC: National Commission on Terrorist Attacks Upon the United States.

NCSA (National Cyber Security Alliance). (2013). Stay safe online. Retrieved from http://staysafeonline.org/stay-safe-online/protect-your-personal-information/id-theft-and-fraud

Newman, G. R., & Clarke, R. V. (2003). *Superhighway robbery: Preventing e-commerce crime*. New York: Routledge.

Ozkan, O. (2013). *A law enforcement perspective to intelligence failure in mass casualty terrorist attacks by global jihadist movements. A comparative study of September 11, 2001 and November 15–20, 2003 attacks*. Dissertation. Newark, NJ: Rutgers University.

PCMAG. (2013a). Botnet. Retrieved July 20, 2013 from http://www.pcmag.com/encyclopedia/term/38866/botnet

PCMAG. (2013b). Patch. Retrieved July 20, 2013 from http://www.pcmag.com/encyclopedia/term/48892/patch.

Perri, F. S., Lichtenwald, T. G., & MacKenzie, P. M. (2009). The evil twins: The crime terror nexus. *Forensic Examiner, 18*(4), 16–29.

Pickert, J. & Sorenson, S. (2013, April 23). Inside reddit's hunt for Boston bombers. *Time*. Retrieved from http://nation.time.com/2013/04/23/inside-reddits-hunt-for-the-boston-bombers/

Reuters. (2005, August 8). Chronology of Iran's nuclear program. *NY Times*. Retrieved from http://www.nytimes.com/2005/08/08/international/08timeline-iran.html?_r=0

Rodoplu, U., Arnold, J. L., Tokyay, R., Ersoy, G., Cetiner, S., & Yücel, T. (2005a). Impact of the terrorist bombings of the Neve Shalom and Beth Israel synagogues on a hospital in Istanbul, Turkey. *Academic Emergency Medicine, 12*(2), 135–139.

Rodoplu, U., Arnold, J. L., Tokyay, R., Ersoy, G., Cetiner, S., & Yücel, T. (2005b). Impact of the terrorist bombings of the Hong Kong Shanghai Bank Corporation headquarters and the British Consulate on two hospitals in Istanbul, Turkey in November, 2003. *Journal of Trauma-Injury Infection and Critical Care, 59*(1), 195–201.

Rosenau, J. N. (2003). *Distant proximities: Dynamics beyond globalization*. Princeton, NJ: Princeton University Press.

Rössel, T. (2011). Post-Stuxnet industrial security issues demand new malware solutions. *Manufacturing Engineering, 146*(5), 30–35.

Rusnak, D. M., Kennedy, L. W., Eldivan, I. S., & Caplan, J. M. (2012). Analyzing terrorism using spatial analysis techniques: A case study of Turkish cities. In C. Lum & L. W. Kennedy (Eds.), *Evidence-based counterterrorism policy* (pp. 167–185). New York: Springer.

Sacco, V., & Kennedy, L. W. (2002). *The criminal event: Explorations in time and space*. Belmont, CA: Wadsworth.

Sacco, V., & Kennedy, L. W. (2010). *The criminal event* (5th ed.). Toronto, ON, Canada: Nelson.

Sanger, D. E. & Schmitt, E. (2012, July 26). Rise is seen in cyberattacks targeting U.S. infrastructure. *NY Times*. Retrieved from http://www.nytimes.com/2012/07/27/us/cyberattacks-are-up-national-security-chief-says.html

Schmid, I. S. (2004). Statistics of terrorism: The challenge of measuring trends, global terrorism. *Forum of Crime and Society, 4*(1–2), 49–69.

Scholte, J. (2005). *Globalization: A critical introduction* (2nd ed.). New York: Palgrave McMillan.

Senay, B. (2008). How do the youth perceive and experience Turkish citizenship. *Middle Eastern Studies, 44*(6), 963–976.

Shearer, J. (2013). W32. Stuxnet. Symantec. Retrieved May 27, 2013 from http://www.symantec.com/security_response/writeup.jsp?docid=2010-071400-3123-99

Sheehan, I. S. (2012). Assessing and comparing data sources for terrorism research. In C. Lum & L. W. Kennedy (Eds.), *Evidence-based counterterrorism policy* (pp. 13–40). New York: Springer.

Shively, K. (2008). Taming Islam: Studying religion in secular Turkey. *Anthropological Quarterly, 81*(3), 683–711.

Sieber, U., & Brunst, P. W. (2007). *Cyberterrorism—The use of the Internet for terrorist purposes*. Washington, DC: Congressional Research Service, Library of Congress.

START. (2011). *Background report: 9/11, Ten years later*. College Park, MD: University of Maryland.

Stouffer, K., Falco, J., & Scarfone, K. (2011). *Guide to industrial control systems (ICS) security*. Gaithersburg, MD: National Institute of Standards and Technology. Retrieved from http://csrc.nist.gov/publications/nistpubs/800-82/SP800-82-final.pdf.

Sullivan, E., Barr, B., & Zezima, K. (2013, April 19). Tamerlan Tsarnaev dead: Boston marathon bombing suspect one dies in shootout (live updates). *Huffington Post*. Retrieved from http://www.huffingtonpost.com/2013/04/19/tamerlan-tsarnaev-dead-boston-bombing-suspect-dies_n_3116056.html

Surowiecki, J. (2013, April 24). The wise way to crowdsource a manhunt. *The New Yorker*. Retrieved from http://www.newyorker.com/online/blogs/comment/2013/04/reddit-tsarnaev-marathon-bombers-wisdom-of-crowds.html?currentPage=all

Terdiman, D. (2012, April 13). Report: Stuxnet delivered to Iranian nuclear plant on thumb drive. *CBS News*. Retrieved from http://www.cbsnews.com/8301-501465_162-57413557-501465/report-stuxnet-delivered-to-iranian-nuclear-plant-on-thumb-drive/

TNP (Turkish National Police) (ND). (2013). International police cooperation on counter-terrorism (CT) in Turkey. Retrieved from http://www.un.org/en/terrorism/ctitf/pdfs/central_asia_turkey.pdf

TRAC (Transactional Records Access Clearinghouse). (2010). *Detention of criminal aliens: What has congress bought*. Syracuse, NY: Syracuse University. Retrieved from http://trac.syr.edu/immigration/reports/224/index.html.

Treverton, G. F., Jones, S. G., Boraz, S., & Lipscy, P. (2006). *Toward a theory of intelligence*. Santa Monica, CA: Rand.

UN News Centre. (2011, March 16). *Growing links between crime and terrorism the focus of UN Forum*. Retrieved from http://www.un.org/apps/news/story.asp?NewsID=37780&Cr=terrorism&Cr1,%20Date%20of%20last%20access:%20July%2024,%202012

UNDP (United Nations Development Programme). (2013, February 17). Afghan national police cadets return home from training in Turkey. UNDP Afghanistan. Retrieved from http://www.undp.org.af/undp/index.php?option=com_content&view=article&id=239%3Aafghan-national-police-cadets-return-home-from-training-in-turkey&catid=30%3Awhat-we-do&Itemid=28

United Nations. (2013). *Global pulse*. Retrieved from www.unglobalpulse.org

United Nations General Assembly, 60th session. (2006, September 20). Resolution 288. The United Nations global counter-terrorism strategy. (A/RES/60/288). Official record. New York.

UNSC (United Nations Security Council). (2001). Resolution 1373. S/RES/1373. Retrieved May 12, 2013 from http://www.un.org/en/sc/ctc/specialmeetings/2012/docs/United%20Nations%20 Security%20Council%20Resolution%201373%20(2001).pdf

USGAO (United States General Accounting Office). (2004, March). Critical infrastructure protection: Challenges and efforts to secure control systems. Report to Congressional Requesters. Retrieved from http://www.gao.gov/new.items/d04354.pdf

Van Brunschot, E. G., & Kennedy, L. W. (2008). *Risk balance and security*. Thousand Oaks, CA: Sage.

Van Brunschot, E. G., & Kennedy, L. W. (2011). The risk of crime, a framework. In L. W. Kennedy & E. F. McGarrell (Eds.), *Crime and terrorism risk studies in criminology and criminal justice* (pp. 7–16). New York: Routledge.

Verdelho, P. (2008). *The effectiveness of international co-operation against cybercrime: Examples of good practice*. Project on Cybercrime of the Council of Europe. Council of Europe. Retrieved May 14, 2013 from http://www.coe.int/t/dghl/cooperation/economiccrime/cybercrime/t-cy/DOC-567study4-Version7_en.PDF

Voloder, L. (2012). Secular citizenship and muslim belonging in Turkey. *Ethnic and Racial Studies., 36*(5), 838–856.

WCVB. (2013, April 18). 'Lord & Taylor' video leads to identification of Boston marathon bombing suspect.. Retrieved May 25, 2013 from http://www.wcvb.com/news/local/metro/-Lord-Taylor-video-leads-to-identification-of-Boston-Marathon-bombing-suspect/-/11971628/19778450/-/idadl6/-/index.html

Whatis.com. (2013). Fast-flux DNS. Retrieved June 29, 2013 from http://whatis.techtarget.com/definition/fast-flux-DNS

White, J. B. (2002). *Islamist mobilization in turkey: A study in vernacular politics*. Seattle, WA: University of Washington Press.

WHO (World Health Organization). (2009). *Pandemic influenza preparedness and response.* Retrieved from http://www.who.int/csr/disease/influenza/PIPGuidance09.pdf

Wilson, C. (2005). *Computer attack and cyberterrorism: Vulnerabilities and policy issues for congress*. Washington, DC: Library of Congress. Retrieved from http://www.history.navy.mil/library/online/computerattack.htm.

Wilson, C. (2008). *Cyberterrorism: Vulnerabilities and policy issues for congress*. Washington, DC: Library of Congress. Retrieved from http://www.dtic.mil/cgi-bin/GetTRDoc?Location=U2&doc=GetTRDoc.pdf&AD=ADA477642.

Wortley, R. & Smallbone, S. (2006). *Child pornography on the Internet*. Center for Problem Oriented Policing. Retrieved from http://www.popcenter.org/problems/child_pornography/print/

Yavuz, U. G. & Yildirim, N. (n.d.) *International Police Cooperation on Counter-Terrorism (CT) in Turkey*. Retrieved May 25, 2013 (http://www.un.org/en/terrorism/ctitf/pdfs/central_asia_turkey.pdf).

Zgoba, K., Witt, P., Dalessandro, M., & Veysey, B. (2008). *Megan's law: Assessing the practical and monetary efficacy*. Trenton, NJ: The Research and Evaluation Unit Office of Policy Planning New Jersey Department of Corrections.

Zhu, B., Joseph, A., & Sastry, S. (2011, October). *Taxonomy of cyber attacks on SCADA Systems*. Proceedings of the 2011 IEEE International Conference on Cyber, Physical, and Social Computing (CPSCom 2011). Dalian, China.

Index

L.W. Kennedy et al., *Translational Criminology and Counterterrorism: Global Threats and Local Responses*, SpringerBriefs in Criminology, DOI 10.1007/978-1-4614-5556-1, © The Author 2014

MIX
Papier aus verantwortungsvollen Quellen
Paper from responsible sources
FSC® C105338

If you have any concerns about our products,
you can contact us on
ProductSafety@springernature.com

In case Publisher is established outside the EU,
the EU authorized representative is:
Springer Nature Customer Service Center GmbH
Europaplatz 3, 69115 Heidelberg, Germany

Printed by Libri Plureos GmbH
in Hamburg, Germany